THE 100 MOST IMPORTANT BIBLE VERSES EVERY LEADER MUST KNOW!

LEADERSHIP

JAY PAYLEITNER

SMITH FREEMAN Publishing

ABOUT THE AUTHOR: JAY PAYLEITNER

Prior to becoming a full-time author and speaker, Jay served as freelance radio producer for Josh McDowell, Chuck Colson, The Salvation Army, Bible League, National Center for Fathering, and others. Jay has sold more than one half-million books including 52 Things Kids Need from a Dad, If God Were Your Life Coach, and What If God Wrote Your Bucket List? He has been a guest multiple times on The Harvest Show, Moody Radio, and Focus on the Family. Jay and his high school sweetheart, Rita, live in the Chicago area where they raised five awesome kids, loved on ten foster babies, and are cherishing grandparenthood. To invite Jay to speak at your corporate or ministry event, go to jaypayleitner.com.

TABLE OF CONTENTS BY TOPIC

INTRODUCTION

How desperately our world needs Christian leaders who are willing to honor God with their service. This generation faces problems that defy easy solutions, yet face them we must. We need leaders whose vision is clear and whose intentions are pure. Daniel writes, "Those who are wise will shine like the brightness of the heavens, and those who lead many to righteousness, like the stars for ever and ever" (12:3 NIV). Hopefully, you are the kind of leader who walks in wisdom as you offer counsel and direction to your family, to your friends, and to your coworkers.

This book contains 100 Bible verses that every Christian leader must know. So, not surprisingly, these verses contain some of the most important truths you'll ever learn. The ideas on these pages will provide wisdom, courage, and energy for your daily journey.

Whether you're a leader at home, at church, at school, or at work, you need and deserve a regularly scheduled conference with your heavenly Father. After all, you are God's emissary, a person charged with molding lives. God takes your leadership duties very seriously, and so should you.

So, if you are fortunate enough to find yourself in the role of leader, accept a hearty congratulations and a profound word of thanks. Remember that God honors your duties just as surely as He offers His loving abundance to you and yours. With God's help, you are destined to reshape eternity. It's a big job, but don't worry: You and God, working together, can handle it.

1
ABUNDANCE

I have come that they may have life,
and that they may have it more abundantly.
JOHN 10:10 NKJV

As a leader who honors Jesus and seeks to follow in His footsteps, you should expect His abundance. Why? Because Christ's promise still rings true; He came to this earth so that we might have life, abundant and eternal. The Son of God walked among us, and endured the ultimate suffering, so that we, His children, might be blessed now and forever. We can claim His abundance by letting Him guide our steps, by letting Him establish our priorities, and by letting Him rule our hearts.

The abundance described in John 10:10 refers to spiritual health, not material wealth. And that's as it should be because spiritual health is far more important, far more meaningful, far more satisfying than the world's brand of prosperity. We mortals often confuse abundance with affluence. God does not. He knows that earthly wealth is fleeting, but spiritual wealth is not.

Today, will you claim the only kind of abundance that really matters? As a Christian leader, will you slow yourself down long enough to ask your heavenly Father for guidance and protection? Will you claim His spiritual riches and experience His peace? You can, and you should. God's abundance is available to all. Accept it, and be blessed.

God loves you and wants you to experience
peace and life—abundant and eternal.
BILLY GRAHAM

Jesus wants Life for us; Life with a capital L.
JOHN ELDREDGE

God is the giver, and we are the receivers. And His richest gifts
are bestowed not upon those who do the greatest things,
but upon those who accept His abundance and His grace.
HANNAH WHITALL SMITH

We honor God by asking for great things when they are a part
of His promise. We dishonor Him and cheat ourselves when we
ask for molehills where He has promised mountains.
VANCE HAVNER

Knowing that your future is absolutely assured
can free you to live abundantly today.
SARAH YOUNG

We shall find in Christ enough of everything we need—
for the body, for the mind, and for the spirit—
to do what He wants us to do as long as He wants us to do it.
VANCE HAVNER

More from God's Word

Until now you have asked for nothing in My name.
Ask and you will receive, that your joy may be complete.
John 16:24 HCSB

And God is able to make all grace abound to you,
so that always having all sufficiency in everything,
you may have an abundance for every good deed.
2 Corinthians 9:8 NASB

Success, success to you, and success to those who help you,
for your God will help you.
1 Chronicles 12:18 NIV

My cup runs over. Surely goodness and mercy
shall follow me all the days of my life;
and I will dwell in the house of the Lord forever.
Psalm 23:5–6 NKJV

The Lord bless you and protect you; the Lord make His face
shine on you, and be gracious to you.
Numbers 6:24–25 HCSB

A Timely Tip for Leaders

God wants to bless you with His abundance and His love; your job is to let Him.

2

ACCEPTANCE

*Should we accept only good things
from the hand of God and never anything bad?*
JOB 2:10 NLT

All of us encounter situations and circumstances that we wish we could change. But we can't. Sometimes, the problems are simply too big for us to solve. Sometimes, the things we regret happened long ago, and no matter how many times we replay the events over in our mind, the past remains unchanged. And sometimes, we're swept up by life-altering events that we simply cannot control.

Reinhold Neibuhr penned a simple verse that has come to be known as the Serenity Prayer. It begins with a brief, yet profound, request: "God, grant me the serenity to accept the things I cannot change." Niebuhr's words are far easier to recite than they are to live by. Why? Because most of us want life to unfold in accordance with in accordance with our own wishes and timetables. But sometimes God has other plans.

If you've a leader who has encountered unfortunate circumstances that are beyond your power to control, accept those circumstances. And trust God. When you do, you can be comforted in the knowledge that your Creator is good, that His love endures forever, and that He understands His plans perfectly, even when you do not.

Christians who are strong in the faith grow as they
accept whatever God allows to enter their lives.
BILLY GRAHAM

Acceptance says, "True, this is my situation at the moment.
I'll look unblinkingly at the reality of it. But, I'll also open
my hands to accept willingly whatever a loving Father sends."
CATHERINE MARSHALL

One of the marks of spiritual maturity is the quiet
confidence that God is in control, without the need
to understand why he does what he does.
CHARLES SWINDOLL

Loving Him means the thankful acceptance
of all things that His love has appointed.
ELISABETH ELLIOT

Accept each day as it comes to you. Do not waste your time
and energy wishing for a different set of circumstances.
SARAH YOUNG

How changed our lives would be if we could only
fly through the days on wings of surrender and trust!
HANNAH WHITALL SMITH

More from God's Word

*Everything God made is good, and nothing should
be refused if it is accepted with thanks.*
1 Timothy 4:4 NCV

He is the Lord. He will do what He thinks is good.
1 Samuel 3:18 HCSB

*Trust in the Lord with all your heart
and lean not on your own understanding....*
Proverbs 3:5 NIV

*For Yahweh is good, and His love is eternal;
His faithfulness endures through all generations.*
Psalm 100:5 HCSB

*For now we see in a mirror, dimly, but then face to face.
Now I know in part, but then I shall know
just as I also am known.*
1 Corinthians 13:12 NKJV

A Timely Tip for Leaders

Think of at least one aspect of your life or your career that you've
been reluctant to accept, and then ask God to help you trust Him
more by accepting the past.

3

ACTION

But prove yourselves doers of the word,
and not merely hearers who delude themselves.
JAMES 1:22 NASB

Leadership requires action. The best leaders don't just talk about getting things done; they manage to get things done, even when it's hard.

When action needs to be taken, the best time to do it is usually now, not later. But we're tempted to do otherwise. When the task at hand is difficult or unpleasant, we're tempted to procrastinate. But procrastination is the enemy of progress and a stumbling block on the path to success.

So, if you if you'd like to jumpstart your career or your life, ask God to give you the strength and the wisdom to do first things first, even if the first thing is hard. And while you're at it, use this time-tested formula for success: less talk and more action. Because actions indeed speak louder than words. And a thousand good intentions pale in comparison to a single good deed.

Action springs not from thought,
but from a readiness for responsibility.
DIETRICH BONHOEFFER

The one word in the spiritual vocabulary is now.
OSWALD CHAMBERS

The world is moving so fast these days that
the one who says it can't be done is generally
interrupted by someone doing it.
HARRY EMERSON FOSDICK

Pray as though everything depended on God.
Work as though everything depended on you.
ST. AUGUSTINE

There's some task which the God of all the universe,
the great Creator has for you to do, and which will
remain undone and incomplete, until by faith and obedience,
you step into the will of God.
ALAN REDPATH

Authentic faith cannot help but act.
BETH MOORE

More from God's Word

For the kingdom of God is not in talk but in power.
1 CORINTHIANS 4:20 HCSB

Therefore, get your minds ready for action, being self-disciplined, and set your hope completely on the grace to be brought to you at the revelation of Jesus Christ.
1 PETER 1:13 HCSB

Whenever we have the opportunity, we should do good to everyone—especially to those in the family of faith.
GALATIANS 6:10 NLT

When you make a vow to God, do not delay in fulfilling it. He has no pleasure in fools; fulfill your vow.
ECCLESIASTES 5:4 NIV

Well done, good and faithful servant; you were faithful over a few things, I will make you ruler over many things. Enter into the joy of your lord.
MATTHEW 25:21 NKJV

A Timely Tip for Leaders

Because actions always speak louder than words, it's always the right time to demonstrate your leadership by letting your actions speak for themselves.

4

ADVERSITY

We are hard-pressed on every side, yet not crushed;
we are perplexed, but not in despair.
2 CORINTHIANS 4:8 NKJV

The times that try men's souls are also the times when character is forged on the anvil of adversity. But the character-building is never easy. Surviving tough times requires courage, strength, prayer, and plenty of hard work.

Elbert Hubbard observed, "When troubles arise, wise men go to their work." Easier said than done. During difficult times, we are tempted to complain, to worry, to blame, and to do little else. Usually, complaints and worries change nothing; intelligent work, on the other hand, changes everything for the better.

During difficult days, even the most dedicated men and women are tempted to lose hope. But we must never abandon our hopes altogether. And we must never stop trusting God, who never gives us heavier burdens than we can bear.

If we are to build better lives for ourselves and our loved ones, we must continue to believe in—and work for—a brighter future. We must not give in; we must persevere. What's required is a combination of faith, work, wisdom, courage, and determination. When we face our challenges with open eyes, courageous hearts, plenty of prayer, and willing hands, miracles happen.

When life kicks you, let it kick you forward.
E. STANLEY JONES

No faith is so precious as that
which triumphs over adversity.
C. H. SPURGEON

God alone can give us songs in the night.
C. H. SPURGEON

God is in control. He may not take away trials
or make detours for us,
but He strengthens us through them.
BILLY GRAHAM

Human problems are never greater than divine solutions.
ERWIN LUTZER

Life is literally filled with God-appointed storms.
These squalls surge across everyone's horizon.
We all need them.
CHARLES SWINDOLL

More from God's Word

I called to the LORD in my distress; I called to my God.
From His temple He heard my voice.
2 SAMUEL 22:7 HCSB

The LORD is my rock, my fortress, and my deliverer, my God,
my mountain where I seek refuge. My shield, the horn of
my salvation, my stronghold, my refuge, and my Savior.
2 SAMUEL 22:2–3 HCSB

God blesses the people who patiently endure testing
and temptation. Afterward they will receive the crown
of life that God has promised to those who love him.
JAMES 1:12 NLT

He heals the brokenhearted and binds up their wounds.
PSALM 147:3 HCSB

The LORD is my shepherd; I shall not want.
PSALM 23:1 KJV

A Timely Tip for Leaders

Tough times are simply opportunities to trust God completely and
to find strength in Him. And remember that hard times can also
be times of intense personal and professional growth.

5

ADVICE, GIVING

Good people's words will help many others.
PROVERBS 10:21 NCV

Wise leaders know how and when to dispense advice. From experience, they know the right thing to say and the right way to say it. Sometimes, the message can be delivered softly; on other occasions, more direct communication is needed. While leadership styles vary, Christian leaders are instructed—and constrained—by the teachings and commandments found in God's Holy Word.

The Bible teaches that we must treat others in the same we that we wish to be treated: with dignity, respect, compassion, and concern. That's how leaders should treat their coworkers.

Today, as you fulfill your duties, consider what it means to be a Christian communicator. Be clear *and* compassionate. Choose your words carefully, and don't say anything to another human being that you wouldn't say if Jesus were standing right by your side . . . because He is.

The true secret of giving advice is,
after you've given it, to be perfectly indifferent
whether it is taken or not.
HANNAH WHITALL SMITH

If you have knowledge,
let others light their candles at it.
THOMAS FULLER

You're never too young to be taught
and never too old to teach.
EDWIN LOUIS COLE

I do not think much of a man who is not
wiser today than he was yesterday.
ABRAHAM LINCOLN

Outstanding leaders go out of their way to boost the
self-esteem of their personnel. If people believe in themselves,
it's amazing what they can accomplish.
SAM WALTON

There is a grace of kind listening,
as well as a grace of kind speaking.
FREDERICK W. FABER

More from God's Word

Let the wise listen and add to their learning,
and let the discerning get guidance.
PROVERBS 1:5 NIV

Wise people can also listen and learn.
PROVERBS 1:5 NCV

The wise store up knowledge, but the mouth
of the fool hastens destruction.
PROVERBS 10:14 HCSB

Walk with the wise and become wise;
associate with fools and get in trouble.
PROVERBS 13:20 NLT

How much better to get wisdom than gold! And to get
understanding is to be chosen rather than silver.
PROVERBS 16:16 NKJV

A Timely Tip for Leaders

If you have an important point to make,
don't try to be subtle or clever. Use a pile driver.
Hit the point once. Then, come back and hit it again.
Then, hit it a third time with a tremendous whack!
WINSTON CHURCHILL

6

ADVICE, TAKING

The wise are glad to be instructed.
PROVERBS 10:8 NLT

Every leader, no matter how wise, needs advisors. We live in a world which is so complicated and so complex that no one is wise enough by himself. We all need trusted counselors to help us think clearly, plan wisely, and implement our plans at the right time, in the right way.

Wise leaders seek counsel from a variety of sources. They are constantly searching for ways to make things better, and they're not afraid of contrary opinions or constructive criticism. In fact, they seek a wide spectrum of ideas, always aware that group-think and popular opinions are often wrong.

So, the next time you're faced with a difficult decision, start by talking things over with God, but don't stop there. As the old saying goes, two heads are, indeed, better than one. And sometimes, three are better than two. And on occasion four are better than . . . well, you get the idea.

Don't be afraid to take advice.
There's always something new to learn.
BABE RUTH

True wisdom is marked by willingness to
listen and a sense of knowing when to yield.
ELIZABETH GEORGE

The one who listens before he talks will succeed.
EDWIN LOUIS COLE

The doorstep of wisdom is a consciousness of ignorance, and the
gateway of perfection is a deep sense of imperfection.
C. H. SPURGEON

Wise people listen to wise instruction,
especially instruction from the Word of God.
WARREN WIERSBE

Not until we have become humble and teachable,
standing in awe of God's holiness and sovereignty,
distrusting our own thoughts, and willing to have our minds
turned upside down, can divine wisdom become ours.
J. I. PACKER

More from God's Word

Plans fail when there is no counsel,
but with many advisers they succeed.
PROVERBS 15:22 HCSB

He whose ear listens to the life-giving reproof
will dwell among the wise.
PROVERBS 15:31 NASB

Get all the advice and instruction you can,
and be wise the rest of your life.
PROVERBS 19:20 NLT

Get wisdom—how much better it is than gold!
And get understanding—it is preferable to silver.
PROVERBS 16:16 HCSB

A Timely Tip for Leaders

If you can't listen to constructive criticism with an open mind, perhaps you've acquired a severe case of old-fashioned stubbornness. If so, ask God to soften your heart, open your ears, and enlighten your mind.

7

ANGER

Everyone must be quick to hear, slow to speak, and slow to anger, for man's anger does not accomplish God's righteousness.
JAMES 1:19–20 HCSB

Wise leaders understand—and the Bible promises—that patience pays and anger costs. Anger is harmful, hurtful, and hazardous to your spiritual health, but in the heat of the battle, you'll be tempted to lose your temper. Hopefully, you'll learn to resist that temptation.

Whenever your thoughts are hijacked by angry emotions, you forfeit the peace and perspective that might otherwise be yours. And to make matters worse, angry thoughts may cause you to behave in irrational, self-destructive ways. As the old saying goes, "Anger is only one letter away from danger."

1 Peter 5:8–9 warns "Stay alert! Watch out for your great enemy, the devil. He prowls around like a roaring lion, looking for someone to devour. Stand firm against him, and be strong in your faith" (NLT). And of this you can be sure: Your adversary will use an impatient and unforgiving heart—and the inevitable anger that dwells within it—to sabotage your life and undermine your faith. To be safe, you must cleanse your heart, and you must forgive. You must say yes to God, yes to mercy, yes to love, yes to patience, and no to anger.

Anger and bitterness—whatever the cause—
only end up hurting us. Turn that anger over to Christ.
BILLY GRAHAM

Hot heads and cold hearts never solved anything.
BILLY GRAHAM

Anger is never without a reason,
but seldom a good one.
BEN FRANKLIN

When angry, count to ten before you speak;
if very angry, a hundred.
THOMAS JEFFERSON

Hence it is not enough to deal with the Temper.
We must go to the source, and change the inmost nature,
and the angry humors will die away of themselves.
HENRY DRUMMOND

Two things a man should never be angry at:
what he can help, and what he cannot help.
THOMAS FULLER

More from God's Word

*But I tell you that anyone who is angry with
a brother or sister will be subject to judgment.*
Matthew 5:22 NIV

*He who is slow to wrath has great understanding,
but he who is impulsive exalts folly.*
Proverbs 14:29 NKJV

*A hot-tempered man stirs up conflict,
but a man slow to anger calms strife.*
Proverbs 15:18 HCSB

*But now you must also put away all the following: anger,
wrath, malice, slander, and filthy language from your mouth.*
Colossians 3:8 HCSB

*Do not let the sun go down on your anger,
and do not give the devil an opportunity.*
Ephesians 4:26–27 NASB

A Timely Tip for Leaders

Angry outbursts can be dangerous to your emotional and
spiritual health, not to mention your personal and professional
relationships. So treat anger as an uninvited guest, and usher it
away as quickly—and as quietly—as possible.

8

ANXIETY AND WORRY

Therefore do not worry about tomorrow,
for tomorrow will worry about its own things.
Sufficient for the day is its own trouble.
MATTHEW 6:34 NKJV

Because we are human beings who have the capacity to think and to anticipate future events, we worry. We worry about big things, little things, and just about everything in between. To make matters worse, we live in a world that breeds anxiety and fosters fear. So it's not surprising that when we come face to face with tough times, we may fall prey to discouragement, doubt, or depression. But our Father in heaven has other plans.

Even the most confident leaders are plagued by the inevitable worries that accompany responsibility. But God has promised that we may lead lives of abundance, not anxiety. In fact, His Word instructs us to "be anxious for nothing." So how can we put our fears to rest? By taking those fears to Him and leaving them there.

The very same God who created the universe has promised to protect you now and forever. So what do you have to worry about? With God on your side, the answer is, "Nothing."

Knowing that God is faithful,
it really helps me to not be captivated by worry.
JOSH McDOWELL

Worry is simply thinking the same thing over and over again . . .
and not doing anything about it.
BRANCH RICKEY

Have courage and do not worry. If you do your best,
never lose your temper, and are never out-fought or out-hustled,
you have nothing to worry about.
But, without faith and courage you are lost.
JOHN WOODEN

Pray, and let God worry.
MARTIN LUTHER

Do not worry about tomorrow.
This is not a suggestion, but a command.
SARAH YOUNG

Today is the tomorrow you worried about yesterday.
BILLY GRAHAM

MORE FROM GOD'S WORD

Let not your heart be troubled;
you believe in God, believe also in Me.
JOHN 14:1 NKJV

Cast all your anxiety on him because he cares for you.
1 PETER 5:7 NIV

Peace I leave with you; My peace I give to you;
not as the world gives do I give to you. Do not
let your heart be troubled, nor let it be fearful.
JOHN 14:27 NASB

Do not be anxious about anything, but in every situation,
by prayer and petition, with thanksgiving,
present your requests to God.
PHILIPPIANS 4:6 NIV

Cast your burden on the LORD, And He shall sustain you;
He shall never permit the righteous to be moved.
PSALM 55:22 NKJV

A TIMELY TIP FOR LEADERS

Divide your areas of concern into two categories: those you can control and those you cannot. Focus on the former and refuse to waste time or energy worrying about the latter.

9

ASKING GOD

Ask, and it will be given to you; seek, and you will find;
knock, and it will be opened to you. For everyone
who asks receives, and he who seeks finds,
and to him who knocks it will be opened.

MATTHEW 7:7–8 NASB

The Lord invites us to pray about the things we need, and He promises to hear our prayers. God is always available, and He's always ready to help us. And He knows precisely what we need, but He still instructs us to ask.

Do you make a habit of asking God for the things you need? Hopefully so. After all, the Father most certainly has a plan for your life. And, He can do great things through you if you have the courage to ask for His guidance and His help. So be fervent in prayer and don't hesitate to ask the Creator for the tools you need to accomplish His plan for your life. Then, get busy and expect the best. When you do your part, God will most certainly do His part. And great things are bound to happen.

We honor God by asking for great things when they are
a part of His promise. We dishonor Him and cheat ourselves
when we ask for molehills where He has promised mountains.
VANCE HAVNER

The easiest way to discover the purpose of an invention
is to ask the creator of it. The same is true for
discovering your life's purpose: Ask God.
RICK WARREN

Are you serious about wanting God's guidance to become a
personal reality in your life? The first step is to tell God that you
know you can't manage your own life; that you need his help.
CATHERINE MARSHALL

God insists that we ask, not because He needs to know our
situation, but because we need the spiritual discipline of asking.
CATHERINE MARSHALL

God will help us become the people we are meant to be,
if only we will ask Him.
HANNAH WHITALL SMITH

When you ask God to do something,
don't ask timidly; put your whole heart into it.
MARIE T. FREEMAN

More from God's Word

Until now you have asked for nothing in My name.
Ask and you will receive, that your joy may be complete.
JOHN 16:24 HCSB

Do not be anxious about anything,
but in every situation, by prayer and petition,
with thanksgiving, present your requests to God.
PHILIPPIANS 4:6 NIV

The effective prayer of a righteous man can accomplish much.
JAMES 5:16 NASB

Your Father knows the things
you have need of before you ask Him.
MATTHEW 6:8 NKJV

You did not choose me, but I chose you
and appointed you so that you might go and bear fruit—
fruit that will last—and so that whatever
you ask in my name the Father will give you.
JOHN 15:16 NIV

A Timely Tip for Leaders

Think of a specific need that is weighing heavily on your heart.
Then, spend a few moments every day asking God for His
guidance and for His help.

10

ATTITUDE

Finally, brothers, rejoice. Become mature, be encouraged,
be of the same mind, be at peace,
and the God of love and peace will be with you.
2 CORINTHIANS 13:11 HCSB

When it comes to leaders, attitude determines altitude: Those with can-do attitudes rise to the top while the naysayers sink.

Attitudes are the mental filters through which we view and interpret the world around us. Your attitude will inevitably determine the quality and direction of your day, your career, and your life. That's why it's so important to stay positive.

The Christian life can be, and should be, cause for celebration. After all, every new day is a gift, every new circumstance an opportunity to praise and to serve. So what's your attitude today? Are you expecting God to do big things in your life and your organization? Are you willing to work hard, work smart, and encourage your co-workers to do likewise? Will you lead the way for others, will you put down stepping stones, not stumbling blocks? If so, your efforts will be rewarded, perhaps sooner than you think.

It's easy to have a great attitude when things are going our way. It's when difficult challenges rise before us that attitude becomes the difference maker.

JOHN MAXWELL

We choose what attitudes we have right now. And it's a continuing choice.

JOHN MAXWELL

The longer I live the more convinced I become that life is 10 percent what happens to us and 90 percent how we respond to it.

CHARLES SWINDOLL

God never promises to remove us from our struggles. He does promise, however, to change the way we look at them.

MAX LUCADO

The past cannot be changed, but one's response to it can be.

ERWIN LUTZER

Your attitude, not your aptitude, will determine your altitude.

ZIG ZIGLAR

More from God's Word

A merry heart makes a cheerful countenance.
PROVERBS 15:13 NKJV

*You must have the same attitude
that Christ Jesus had.*
PHILIPPIANS 2:5 NLT

*Be glad and rejoice, because
your reward is great in heaven.*
MATTHEW 5:12 HCSB

Rejoice always; pray without ceasing.
1 THESSALONIANS 5:16–17 NASB

*This is the day the LORD has made;
let us rejoice and be glad in it.*
PSALM 118:24 HCSB

A Timely Tip for Leaders

As a Christian leader, you have every reason on earth—and in heaven—to have a positive attitude. After all, God's in charge, He loves you, and He's prepared a place for you to live eternally with Him. And that's what really matters.

11
BEGINNING

Do not remember the former things, nor consider
the things of old. Behold, I will do a new thing.
ISAIAH 43:18–19 NKJV

Sometimes, the hardest thing is to begin. We have high hopes, big dreams, and grand plans. But somehow, we never manage to move from the planning stage to the action stage. Meanwhile, as we play it safe and wait for the "perfect" time to start, the clock continues to tick as days turn into weeks, then months, then years.

Do you have an exciting plan that you haven't yet acted upon? Are you playing it safe, perhaps too safe, by waiting for the ideal moment before you begin? If so, you may be missing important opportunities.

Norman Vincent Peale correctly observed that, "Great things develop from small beginnings." Walt Disney advised, "The way to get started is to stop talking and start doing." And Andrew Carnegie warned, "The first man gets the oyster. The second man gets the shell." All three men were right. Procrastination can be expensive, sometimes very expensive. So if you've been putting off your next grand adventure, it's probably time to reorder your to-do list. The best day to begin an important task is this day. Tomorrow, or the next day, or the next, may be too late.

God specializes in giving people a fresh start.
RICK WARREN

What saves a man is to take a step.
Then another step.
C. S. LEWIS

The best preparation for the future
is the present well seen to,
and the last duty done.
GEORGE MACDONALD

Are you in earnest? Seize this very minute.
What you can do, or dream you can, begin it.
Boldness has genius, power, and magic in it.
GOETHE

In one bold stroke, forgiveness obliterates the past
and permits us to enter the land of new beginnings.
BILLY GRAHAM

MORE FROM GOD'S WORD

Your old sinful self has died,
and your new life is kept with Christ in God.
COLOSSIANS 3:3 NCV

You are being renewed in the spirit of your minds;
you put on the new self, the one created according to God's
likeness in righteousness and purity of the truth.
EPHESIANS 4:23–24 HCSB

There is one thing I always do. Forgetting the past and
straining toward what is ahead, I keep trying to reach the goal
and get the prize for which God called me.
PHILIPPIANS 3:13–14 NCV

Then the One seated on the throne said,
"Look! I am making everything new."
REVELATION 21:5 HCSB

"For I know the plans I have for you"—
this is the LORD's declaration—"plans for your welfare,
not for disaster, to give you a future and a hope."
JEREMIAH 29:11 HCSB

A TIMELY TIP FOR LEADERS

If you're graduating into a new phase of life, be sure to make God
your partner. If you do, He'll guide your steps; He'll help carry
your burdens; He'll help you become a better leader; and, He'll
help you focus on the things that really matter.

12

BEHAVIOR

Now by this we know that we know Him,
if we keep His commandments.
1 JOHN 2:3 NKJV

It's always been true: Actions, indeed, speak louder than words. No matter how loudly we proclaim our love for the Lord, our actions reveal our true priorities. As Thomas Fuller observed, "He does not believe who does not live according to his beliefs."

Every day, we make decisions that can bring us closer to God, or not. When we follow closely in the footsteps of Christ, we experience His abundance and His peace. But, when we stray far from God's path, we bring needless pain and suffering upon ourselves and our families.

Do you want to experience God's peace and His blessings? Then obey Him. When you do, you will be blessed today, and tomorrow, and forever.

Resolved, never to do anything which I
would be afraid to do if it were the last hour of my life.
JONATHAN EDWARDS

Never support an experience which does not have God
as its source and faith in God as its result.
OSWALD CHAMBERS

There are two things to do about the Gospel:
believe it and behave it.
SUSANNA WESLEY

One of the real tests of Christian character
is to be found in the lives we live from day to day.
BILLY GRAHAM

Our battles are first won or lost in the secret places of our will
in God's presence, never in full view of the world.
OSWALD CHAMBERS

It is not your business to succeed, but to do right:
when you have done so, the rest lies with God.
C. S. LEWIS

More from God's Word

*Walk in a manner worthy of the God who
calls you into His own kingdom and glory.*
1 Thessalonians 2:12 NASB

Live peaceful and quiet lives in all godliness and holiness.
1 Timothy 2:2 NIV

*But prove yourselves doers of the word,
and not merely hearers who delude themselves.*
James 1:22 NASB

*To do evil is like sport to a fool,
but a man of understanding has wisdom.*
Proverbs 10:23 NKJV

In everything set them an example by doing what is good.
Titus 2:7 NIV

A Timely Tip for Leaders

Ask yourself if your behavior and your leadership skills have been
radically changed by your unfolding relationship with God. If the
answer is unclear to you—or if the answer is no—think of a single
step you can take, a positive change, that will bring you closer to
your Creator.

13
BELIEF

I have come as a light into the world, that whoever
believes in Me should not abide in darkness.
JOHN 12:46 NKJV

Talking about our beliefs is easy; living by them is considerably harder. Yet God warns us that speaking about faith is not enough; we must also live by faith. Simply put, our theology must be demonstrated, not only with words but, more importantly, with actions.

As Christians, our instructions are clear: We should trust God's plan, obey God's Word, and follow God's Son. When we do these things, we inevitably partake in the spiritual abundance that the Creator has promised to those who walk in the light. But if we listen to God's instructions on Sunday morning but ignore them the rest of the week, we'll pay a heavy price for our misplaced priorities.

Every new day presents fresh opportunities to ensure that your actions are consistent with your beliefs. As a Christian leader, you owe it to yourself and your coworkers to seize those opportunities. Now.

What I believe about God
is the most important thing about me.
A. W. TOZER

He does not believe who does not live according to his beliefs.
THOMAS FULLER

It is an act of simplicity to choose to believe God, but it is
also is an act of profound complexity as God literally moves in
wondrous ways throughout the universe to keep His word.
BILL BRIGHT

Only believe, don't fear. Our Master, Jesus,
always watches over us, and no matter what the persecution,
Jesus will surely overcome it.
LOTTIE MOON

Unless he obeys, a man cannot believe.
DIETRICH BONHOEFFER

A person's beliefs hold the greatest potential
for good or harm in life.
EDWIN LOUIS COLE

More from God's Word

*Jesus said, "Because you have seen Me, you have believed.
Those who believe without seeing are blessed."*
JOHN 20:29 HCSB

*I tell you the truth, whoever believes in me will do the same
things that I do. Those who believe will do even greater things
than these, because I am going to the Father.*
JOHN 14:12 NCV

*Most assuredly, I say to you, he who believes in Me,
the works that I do he will do also.*
JOHN 14:12 NKJV

All things are possible for the one who believes.
MARK 9:23 NCV

*I know the One I have believed in and am persuaded that He is
able to guard what has been entrusted to me until that day.*
2 TIMOTHY 1:12 HCSB

A Timely Tip for Leaders

If you stand up for your beliefs—and when you follow your
conscience—you'll make better decisions, and you'll be a better
leader.

14

BIBLE STUDY

*All scripture is given by inspiration of God,
and is profitable for doctrine, for reproof, for correction,
for instruction in righteousness.*

2 TIMOTHY 3:16 KJV

The promises found in God's Word are the cornerstone of the Christian faith. We must trust those promises and build our lives upon them.

The Bible is a priceless gift—a tool for Christians to use every day, in every situation. Yet too many leaders put away their spiritual toolkits and rely, instead, on the world's promises. Unfortunately, the world makes promises it doesn't keep. God has no such record of failure. He keeps every single one of His promises. On Him you can depend.

So how will you, as a Christian Leader, respond to God's promises? Will you treat your Bible as a one-of-a-kind guidebook for life here on earth and life eternal in heaven? And, will you let your Creator speak to you through His Holy Word? Hopefully so because the Lord has given you all the tools you need to accomplish His plan for your life. He placed every instruction you'll need in the book He wrote. The rest is up to you.

Reading the Bible has a purifying effect upon your life.
Let nothing take the place of this daily exercise.
BILLY GRAHAM

Do you want your faith to grow? Then let the Bible
began to saturate your mind and soul.
BILLY GRAHAM

Gather the riches of God's promises.
Nobody can take away from you those texts from the Bible
which you have learned by heart.
CORRIE TEN BOOM

Read the scripture, not only as history,
but as a love letter sent to you from God.
THOMAS WATSON

When you read the Bible, read for quality not quantity.
ADRIAN ROGERS

When you read God's word, you must
constantly be saying to yourself,
"It is talking to me and about me."
SØREN KIERKEGAARD

More from God's Word

The counsel of the LORD stands forever,
the plans of His heart from generation to generation.
PSALM 33:11 NASB

But the word of the Lord endures forever. And this is the word
that was preached as the gospel to you.
1 PETER 1:25 HCSB

But whoever looks intently into the perfect law that gives
freedom, and continues in it—not forgetting what they have
heard, but doing it—they will be blessed in what they do.
JAMES 1:25 NIV

But grow in the grace and knowledge
of our Lord and Savior Jesus Christ. To Him be the glory
both now and to the day of eternity.
2 PETER 3:18 HCSB

You will be a good servant of Christ Jesus,
nourished by the words of the faith
and the good teaching that you have followed.
1 TIMOTHY 4:6 HCSB

A Timely Tip for Leaders

Even if you've studied the Bible for many years, you've still got lots to learn. Bible study should be a lifelong endeavor. Make it your lifelong endeavor.

15

BITTERNESS

Let all bitterness, wrath, anger, clamor, and evil speaking
be put away from you, with all malice.
And be kind to one another, tenderhearted,
forgiving one another, just as God in Christ forgave you.
EPHESIANS 4:31–32 NKJV

Bitterness is a spiritual sickness. It will consume your soul; it is dangerous to your emotional health; it can destroy you if you let it. So don't let it!

The world holds few if any rewards for leaders who remain angrily focused upon the past. Still, the act of forgiveness is difficult for all but the most saintly men and women. Being frail, fallible, imperfect human beings, most of us are quick to anger, quick to blame, slow to forgive, and even slower to forget. Yet we know that it's best to forgive others, just as we, too, have been forgiven.

If there exists even one person—including yourself—against whom you still harbor bitter feelings, it's time to forgive and move on. Bitterness, and regret are not part of God's plan for you, but God won't force you to forgive others. It's a job that only you can finish, and the sooner you finish it, the better.

If you are caught up in intense feelings of anger or resentment, you know all too well the destructive power of these emotions. How can you rid yourself of these feelings? First, you must prayerfully ask God to cleanse your heart. Then, you must learn to catch yourself whenever thoughts of bitterness or hatred begin to attack you. Your challenge is this: You must learn to resist negative thoughts before they hijack your emotions. When you learn to direct your thoughts toward more positive, topics, you'll be protected from the spiritual and emotional consequences of bitterness. And you'll be wiser, healthier, and happier, too.

Bitterness imprisons life; love releases it.
HARRY EMERSON FOSDICK

Bitterness sentences you to relive the hurt over and over.
LEE STROBEL

Bitterness is anger gone sour, an attitude
of deep discontent that poisons our souls
and destroys our peace.
BILLY GRAHAM

Bitterness imprisons life; love releases it.
HARRY EMERSON FOSDICK

Give me such love for God and men
as will blot out all hatred and bitterness.
DIETRICH BONHOEFFER

He who cannot forgive others breaks the bridge
over which he himself must pass.
CORRIE TEN BOOM

More from God's Word

Do all things without complaining and disputing,
that you may become blameless and harmless, children of God
without fault in the midst of a crooked and perverse generation,
among whom you shine as lights in the world.
PHILIPPIANS 2:14–15 NKJV

Do not repay anyone evil for evil.
Try to do what is honorable in everyone's eyes.
ROMANS 12:17 HCSB

But when you are praying, first forgive
anyone you are holding a grudge against, so that
your Father in heaven will forgive your sins, too.
MARK 11:25 NLT

The heart knows its own bitterness,
and a stranger does not share its joy.
PROVERBS 14:10 NKJV

Do not judge, and you will not be judged.
Do not condemn, and you will not be condemned.
Forgive, and you will be forgiven.
LUKE 6:37 HCSB

A Timely Tip for Leaders

The Bible warns that bitterness is both dangerous and self-destructive. So today, make a list of the people you need to forgive and the things you need to forget. Then, ask God to give you the strength to forgive and move on.

16

BLESSINGS

The Lord bless you and protect you; the Lord
make His face shine on you, and be gracious to you.
NUMBERS 6:24–25 HCSB

Each of us has much to be thankful for. We all have more blessings than we can count, beginning with the precious gift of life. Every good gift comes from our Father above, and we owe Him our never-ending thanks. But sometimes, when the demands of everyday life press down upon us, we neglect to express our gratitude to the Creator.

God loves us; He cares for us; He has a plan for each of us; and, He has offered us the gift of eternal life through His Son. Considering all the things that the Lord has done, we owe it to Him—and to ourselves—to slow down many times each day and offer our thanks. His grace is everlasting; our thanks should be, too.

God loves you and wants you to experience
peace and life—abundant and eternal.
BILLY GRAHAM

God is always trying to give good things to us,
but our hands are too full to receive them.
ST. AUGUSTINE

All the blessings we enjoy are Divine deposits,
committed to our trust on this condition, that they
should be dispensed for the benefit of our neighbors.
JOHN CALVIN

Every difficult task that comes across your path—
every one that you would rather not do, that will
take the most effort, cause the most pain,
and be the greatest struggle—brings a blessing with it.
LETTIE COWMAN

The only way you can experience abundant life
is to surrender your plans to Him.
CHARLES STANLEY

Jesus wants Life for us; Life with a capital L.
JOHN ELDREDGE

MORE FROM GOD'S WORD

You will show me the path of life; in Your presence is
fullness of joy; at Your right hand are pleasures forevermore.
PSALM 16:11 NKJV

The LORD is good to all: and his
tender mercies are over all his works.
PSALM 145:9 KJV

The LORD is my rock, my fortress, and my deliverer, my God,
my mountain where I seek refuge. My shield, the horn of
my salvation, my stronghold, my refuge, and my Savior.
2 SAMUEL 22:2–3 HCSB

The LORD is my shepherd;
I shall not want.
PSALM 23:1 KJV

Blessings crown the head of the righteous.
PROVERBS 10:6 NIV

A TIMELY TIP FOR LEADERS

God gives us countless blessings. We, in turn, should count
them. And, we should give the Lord the thanks and the praise He
deserves. Wise leaders understand that it pays to praise.

17
CHANGE

To every thing there is a season,
and a time to every purpose under the heaven.
ECCLESIASTES 3:1 KJV

Here in the twenty-first century, change is a fact of life. The world keeps changing and so do we. The question, of course, is whether the changes that *we* initiate turn out to be improvements or impediments. To find the answer to that question, we must first consult a source of wisdom that does not change. That source is God.

God's Word makes it clear: "I am the LORD, I do not change" (Malachi 3:6 NKJV). We can be comforted by the knowledge that our covenant with the Creator is everlasting and non-negotiable. The Lord has promised to keep His word, and that's precisely what He will do.

So, the next time you face tough times or unwelcome changes, remember that one thing never changes: God's love for you. Then, perhaps, you'll worry less, do your best, and leave the rest up to Him.

To improve is to change; to succeed is to change often.
WINSTON CHURCHILL

Change always starts in your mind.
The way you think determines the way you feel,
and the way you feel influences the way you act.
RICK WARREN

Are you on the eve of change? Embrace it. Accept it.
Don't resist it. Change is not only a part of life,
change is a necessary part of God's strategy. To use us
to change the world, he alters our assignments.
MAX LUCADO

Grace is the voice that calls us to change
and then gives us the power to pull it off.
MAX LUCADO

We all want progress, but if you're on the wrong road,
progress means doing an about-turn and
walking back to the right road; in that case, the man
who turns back soonest is the most progressive.
C. S. LEWIS

The world changes—circumstances change, we change—
but God's Word never changes.
WARREN WIERSBE

More from God's Word

The wise see danger ahead and avoid it,
but fools keep going and get into trouble.
PROVERBS 22:3 NCV

But grow in the grace and knowledge
of our Lord and Savior Jesus Christ.
To Him be the glory both now and forever. Amen.
2 PETER 3:18 NKJV

When I was a child, I spoke like a child,
I thought like a child, I reasoned like a child.
When I became a man, I put aside childish things.
1 CORINTHIANS 13:11 HCSB

Then He who sat on the throne said,
"Behold, I make all things new."
REVELATION 21:5 NKJV

I am the LORD, and I do not change.
MALACHI 3:6 NLT

A Timely Tip for Leaders

Change is inevitable. You can either roll with it or be rolled over
by it. As a savvy leader, you must choose the former.

18

CHARACTER, HONESTY, AND INTEGRITY

Whoever walks in integrity walks securely,
but whoever takes crooked paths will be found out.
PROVERBS 10:9 NIV

Christian leaders know that integrity matters. Honesty enriches relationships and builds organizations; deception destroys them.

Henry Blackaby observed, "God is interested in developing your character. At times He lets you proceed, but He will never let you go too far without discipline to bring you back." The implication is clear: Personal integrity is important to God, so it must be important to us.

Living a life of integrity isn't the easiest way, but it's always the best way. So if you find yourself tempted to break the truth—or to bend it—remember that honesty is, indeed, the best policy; it's also God's policy; so, it must be your policy, too.

Character is both developed and revealed by tests,
and all of life is a test.
RICK WARREN

True greatness is not measured by the headlines or wealth.
The inner character of a person is
the true measure of lasting greatness.
BILLY GRAHAM

Character is what you are in the dark.
D. L. MOODY

Remember that your character is the sum total of your habits.
RICK WARREN

Give to us clear vision that we may know
where to stand and what to stand for—because
unless we stand for something, we shall fall for anything.
PETER MARSHALL

What happens outwardly in your life is not as
important as what happens inside you. Your circumstances
are temporary, but your character will last forever.
RICK WARREN

More from God's Word

The integrity of the upright guides them,
but the perversity of the treacherous destroys them.
PROVERBS 11:3 HCSB

The godly are directed by their honesty.
PROVERBS 11:5 NLT

He stores up success for the upright; He is a shield
for those who live with integrity.
PROVERBS 2:7 HCSB

The godly walk with integrity;
blessed are their children who follow them.
PROVERBS 20:7 NLT

Let integrity and uprightness preserve me,
for I wait for You.
PSALM 25:21 NKJV

A Timely Tip for Leaders

Integrity is more important than popularity. Always has been. Always will be. Live accordingly.

19

CHARITY AND GENEROSITY

Freely you have received, freely give.
MATTHEW 10:8 NIV

The theme of generosity is woven into the fabric of God's Word. Our Creator instructs us to give generously—and cheerfully—to those in need. And He promises that when we do give of our time, our talents, and our resources, we will be blessed.

Jesus was the perfect example of generosity. He gave us everything, even His earthly life, so that we, His followers, might receive abundance, peace, and eternal life. He was always generous, always kind, always willing to help "the least of these." And, if we are to follow in His footsteps, we, too, must be generous.

Sometime today, you'll encounter someone who needs a helping hand or a word of encouragement. When you encounter a person in need, think of yourself as Christ's ambassador. And remember that whatever you do for the least of these, you also do for Him.

The world asks, "What does a man own?"
Christ asks, "How does he use it?"
ANDREW MURRAY

We are never more like God than when we give.
CHARLES SWINDOLL

Christian life consists in faith and charity.
MARTIN LUTHER

In Jesus the service of God and the service
of the least of the brethren were one.
DIETRICH BONHOEFFER

It's what you sow that multiplies,
not what you keep in the barn.
ADRIAN ROGERS

Find out how much God has given you
and from it take what you need;
the remainder is needed by others.
ST. AUGUSTINE

More from God's Word

So let each one give as he purposes in his heart,
not grudgingly or of necessity;
for God loves a cheerful giver.
2 CORINTHIANS 9:7 NKJV

You should remember the words of the Lord Jesus:
"It is more blessed to give than to receive."
ACTS 20:35 NLT

If you have two shirts, give one to the poor. If you have food,
share it with those who are hungry.
LUKE 3:11 NLT

Whenever we have the opportunity, we should do good to
everyone—especially to those in the family of faith.
GALATIANS 6:10 NLT

Truly I tell you, whatever you did for one of the least of these
these brothers and sisters of mine, you did for me.
MATTHEW 25:40 NIV

A Timely Tip for Leaders

There's a direct relationship between generosity and joy; the more
you share with others, the more joy you'll experience for yourself.

20

CHRIST'S LOVE

*As the Father loved Me, I also
have loved you; abide in My love.*
JOHN 15:9 NKJV

On a faraway hill, Jesus was crucified. At noon, darkness came over the land; the curtain of the temple was torn in two; and finally Jesus called out, 'Father, into Your hands I commit My spirit.' Having said this, He breathed His last." (Luke 23:46 NKJV). Christ had endured the crucifixion, and it was finished.

The body was wrapped in a linen shroud and placed in a new tomb. It was there that God breathed life into His Son. It was there that Christ was resurrected. It was there that the angels rejoiced. And it was there, that God's plan for the salvation of mankind was made complete.

As we consider Christ's sacrifice on the cross, we should be profoundly grateful. The Son of God wore a crown of thorns for all humanity. And He did it for you.

Christ humbly shed His blood for you. He has offered to walk with you through this life and throughout all eternity. As you approach Him today in prayer, think about His sacrifice and His grace. And be thankful.

When we open our hearts to Jesus and walk in His footsteps, our lives bear testimony to His mercy and to His grace. Yes, Christ's love changes everything. May we welcome Him into our hearts so that He can then change everything in us.

*Above all else, the Christian life
is a love affair of the heart.*
JOHN ELDREDGE

Jesus: the proof of God's love.
PHILLIP YANCEY

Jesus is all compassion. He never betrays us.
CATHERINE MARSHALL

*As the love of a husband for his bride,
such is the love of Christ for His people.*
C. H. SPURGEON

*Tell me the story of Jesus. Write on my heart
every word. Tell me the story most precious,
sweetest that ever was heard.*
FANNY CROSBY

*To God be the glory, great things He has done.
So loved He the world that He gave us His Son.*
FANNY CROSBY

MORE FROM GOD'S WORD

*I am the good shepherd. The good shepherd
lays down his life for the sheep.*
JOHN 10:11 HCSB

*No one has greater love than this, that someone
would lay down his life for his friends.*
JOHN 15:13 HCSB

*For Christ also suffered once for sins, the just for the unjust,
that He might bring us to God, being put to death in the flesh
but made alive by the Spirit.*
1 PETER 3:18 NKJV

We love him, because he first loved us.
1 JOHN 4:19 KJV

*For God so loved the world, that he gave his
only begotten Son, that whosoever believeth in him
should not perish, but have everlasting life.*
JOHN 3:16 KJV

A TIMELY TIP FOR LEADERS

Christ's love is meant to be experienced—and shared—by you.
As a Christian leader, you should serve your Savior by serving His
children.

21
CHURCH

I was glad when they said unto me,
Let us go into the house of the LORD.
PSALM 122:1 KJV

Every church needs leaders, Christian men and women who understand the importance of sustaining—and being sustained by—their local congregations. In the book of Acts, Luke instructs us to "feed the church of God" (20:28). As Christians who have been given so much by our loving heavenly Father, we should worship Him not only in our hearts but also in the presence of fellow believers.

Today, like every other day, is a wonderful day to honor God by supporting His church. The needs are great; the laborers are few; the time for action is now; and, the blessings are real.

Church-goers are like coals in a fire.
When they cling together, they keep the flame aglow;
when they separate, they die out.
BILLY GRAHAM

Every believer is commanded to
be plugged in to a local church.
DAVID JEREMIAH

The church is a hospital for sinners,
not a museum for saints.
VANCE HAVNER

The Church will outlive the universe;
in it the individual person will outlive the universe.
C. S. LEWIS

The church's job is to equip the saints
for works of service in the world.
CHARLES COLSON

The Bible knows nothing of solitary religion.
JOHN WESLEY

More from God's Word

Be on guard for yourselves and for all the flock that the Holy Spirit has appointed you to as overseers,, to shepherd the church of God, which He purchased with His own blood.

ACTS 20:28 HCSB

For where two or three come together in my name, there am I with them.

MATTHEW 18:20 NIV

Enter his gates with thanksgiving, go into his courts with praise. Give thanks to him and bless his name.

PSALM 100:4 NLT

God is spirit, and those who worship Him must worship in spirit and truth.

JOHN 4:24 HCSB

Worship the Lord your God, and serve only Him.

MATTHEW 4:10 HCSB

A Timely Tip for Leaders

Your church needs you. What you put into church determines what you get out of it. Your attitude towards worship is vitally important, so celebrate accordingly.

22

CIRCUMSTANCES

*Trust in him at all times, you people; pour out
your hearts to him, for God is our refuge.*
PSALM 62:8 NIV

From time to time, all of us must endure unpleasant circumstances. We find ourselves in situations that we didn't ask for and probably don't deserve. During these times, we try our best to "hold up under the circumstances." But God has a better plan. He intends for us to rise above our circumstances, and He's promised to help us do it.

Are you a leader who's dealing with a difficult situation or a tough problem? Do you struggle with occasional periods of discouragement and doubt? Are you worried, weary, or downcast? If so, don't face tough times alone. Face them with God as your partner, your protector, and your guide. When you do, He will give you the strength meet any challenge, the courage to face any problem, and the patience to endure any circumstance.

God has a purpose behind every problem.
He uses circumstances to develop our character.
RICK WARREN

Oftentimes God demonstrates His faithfulness in adversity by
providing for us what we need to survive. He does not change
our painful circumstances. He sustains us through them.
CHARLES STANLEY

Worship God in the difficult circumstances,
and when He chooses, He will alter them in two seconds.
OSWALD CHAMBERS

Don't let obstacles along the road to eternity
shake your confidence in God's promises.
DAVID JEREMIAH

Accept each day as it comes to you.
Do not waste your time and energy
wishing for a different set of circumstances.
SARAH YOUNG

No matter what our circumstance,
we can find a reason to be thankful.
DAVID JEREMIAH

MORE FROM GOD'S WORD

The LORD is a refuge for His people and a stronghold.
JOEL 3:16 NASB

The LORD is a refuge for the oppressed,
a refuge in times of trouble.
PSALM 9:9 HCSB

Cast your burden on the LORD, and He shall sustain you;
He shall never permit the righteous to be moved.
PSALM 55:22 NKJV

God is our protection and our strength.
He always helps in times of trouble.
PSALM 46:1 NCV

I have learned in whatever state I am, to be content.
PHILIPPIANS 4:11 NKJV

A TIMELY TIP FOR LEADERS

A change of circumstances is rarely as important as a change in attitude. If you change your thoughts, you will most certainly change your circumstances.

23

COMMUNICATION

A word fitly spoken is like apples of gold in settings of silver.
PROVERBS 25:11 NKJV

More often than not, great leaders are also great communicators. They understand their audience; they understand the message they want to convey; and, they understand how best to convey it.

Christian leaders are bound, not only by the principles of good leadership, but also—and more importantly—by the principles found in God's Holy Word. So, great Christian communicators should convey their messages with humility, with integrity, and with love.

Edwin Louis Cole had simple yet profound advice for Christian leaders in every walk of life. He said, "The truth must be spoken with love." So, if you want to be an effective leader, you must learn how to be truthful without being cruel. You have the power to lift your coworkers up or to hold them back. When you learn how to lift them up, truthfully and compassionately, you'll lift yourself up, too.

It's not what you tell them; it's what they hear.
RED AUERBACH

Make it clear. Make it simple. Emphasize the essentials.
Forget about impressing. Leave some things unsaid.
Let the thing be simplified.
CHARLES SWINDOLL

Put your information across slowly and repeat it
over and over again! Take a difficult point and make it
so simple that it will become clear even to the dullard.
KNUTE ROCKNE

A vocabulary of truth and simplicity
will be of service throughout life.
WINSTON CHURCHILL

Watch your words diligently. Words have such great
power to bless or to wound. When you speak carelessly
or negatively, you damage others as well as yourself.
SARAH YOUNG

If you have an important point to make,
don't try to be subtle or clever. Use a pile driver.
Hit the point once. Then, come back and hit it again.
Then, hit it a third time with a tremendous whack!
WINSTON CHURCHILL

More from God's Word

The heart of the wise teaches his mouth,
and adds learning to his lips.
PROVERBS 16:23 NKJV

Pleasant words are a honeycomb:
sweet to the taste and health to the body.
PROVERBS 16:24 HCSB

If anyone thinks he is religious without controlling his tongue,
then his religion is useless and he deceives himself.
JAMES 1:26 HCSB

What you have said in the dark will be heard in the light,
and what you have whispered in an inner room
will be shouted from the housetops.
LUKE 12:3 NCV

But encourage each other daily, while it is still called today,
so that none of you is hardened by sin's deception.
HEBREWS 3:13 HCSB

A Timely Tip for Leaders

Don't hedge the truth, don't omit important facts, and don't make promises that you can't keep. If you shade the truth, people will always find out anyway . . . and they will always remember.

24

CONFIDENCE

So we may boldly say: "The LORD is my helper;
I will not fear. What can man do to me?"
HEBREWS 13:6 NKJV

As a leader, you need to display confidence—confidence in yourself, confidence in your plan, confidence in your team. And, as a Christian, you have every reason to live confidently. After all, you've read God's promises, and you know that He's prepared a place for you in heaven. And with God on your side, what should you fear? The answer, of course, is, "Nothing." But sometimes, despite your faith and despite God's promises, you find yourself gripped by earthly apprehensions.

When we focus on our doubts and fears, we can concoct a lengthy list of reasons to lie awake at night and fret about the uncertainties of the coming day. A better strategy, of course, is to focus, not upon our fears, but instead upon our God.

Are you a confident Christian? You should be. God's promises never fail and His love is everlasting. So the next time you need a boost of confidence, slow down and have a little chat with your Creator. Count your blessings, not your troubles. Focus on possibilities, not problems. And remember that with God on your side, you have absolutely nothing to fear.

He who has confidence in himself will lead the rest.
HORACE BUSHNELL

You need to make the right decision—
firmly and decisively—
and then stick with it, with God's help.
BILLY GRAHAM

Believe you can and you are halfway there.
THEODORE ROOSEVELT

Confidence in the natural world is self-reliance;
in the spiritual world, it is God-reliance.
OSWALD CHAMBERS

We never get anywhere—nor do our conditions and
circumstances change—when we look at the dark side of life.
LETTIE COWMAN

What think we of Christ? Is He altogether
glorious in our eyes, and precious to our hearts?
May Christ be our joy, our confidence, our all.
MATTHEW HENRY

More from God's Word

You are my hope; O Lord GOD, You are my confidence.
PSALM 71:5 NASB

*I lift up my eyes to the mountains—where does
my help come from? My help comes from the LORD,
the Maker of heaven and earth.*
PSALM 121:1–2 NIV

*God is our refuge and strength,
a very present help in trouble.*
PSALM 46:1 NKJV

*Be strong and courageous, and do the work.
Don't be afraid or discouraged, for the LORD God, my God,
is with you. He won't leave you or forsake you.*
1 CHRONICLES 28:20 HCSB

*In this world you will have trouble.
But take heart! I have overcome the world.*
JOHN 16:33 NIV

A Timely Tip for Leaders

As a Christian leader, you have every reason to be confident. With God as your partner, you have nothing to fear.

25

CONSCIENCE

Now the goal of our instruction is love from a pure heart,
a good conscience, and a sincere faith.
1 TIMOTHY 1:5 HCSB

God has given each of us a conscience, and He intends for us to use it. But sometimes we don't. Instead of listening to that quiet inner voice that warns us against disobedience and danger, we're tempted to rush headlong into situations that we soon come to regret.

God promises that He rewards good conduct and that He blesses those who obey His Word. The Lord also issues a stern warning to those who rebel against His commandments. Wise leaders heed that warning. Count yourself among their number.

Sometime soon, perhaps today, your conscience will speak; when it does, listen carefully. God may be trying to get a message through to you. Don't miss it.

Conscience is God's voice to the inner man.
BILLY GRAHAM

*The conscience is a built-in warning system that signals us
when something we have done is wrong.*
JOHN MACARTHUR

*God speaks through a variety of means.
In the present God primarily speaks by the Holy Spirit,
through the Bible, prayer, circumstances, and the church.*
HENRY BLACKABY

It is neither safe nor prudent to do anything against conscience.
MARTIN LUTHER

Conscience can only be satisfied if God is satisfied.
C. H. SPURGEON

*Conscience is our wisest counselor and teacher,
our most faithful and most patient friend.*
BILLY GRAHAM

More from God's Word

*So I strive always to keep my conscience
clear before God and man.*
ACTS 24:16 NIV

*Let us come near to God with a sincere heart and a sure faith,
because we have been made free from a guilty conscience, and
our bodies have been washed with pure water.*
HEBREWS 10:22 NCV

*People's thoughts can be like a deep well, but someone with
understanding can find the wisdom there.*
PROVERBS 20:5 NCV

*Create in me a clean heart, O God;
and renew a right spirit within me.*
PSALM 51:10 KJV

Behold, the kingdom of God is within you.
LUKE 17:21 KJV

A Timely Tip for Leaders

If you're not sure what to do, slow down and listen to your
conscience. That quiet voice inside your head is remarkably
dependable, but you can't depend upon it if you're too busy to
listen.

26

COOPERATION AND TEAMWORK

You're blessed when you can show people how to cooperate instead of compete or fight. That's when you discover who you really are, and your place in God's family.

MATTHEW 5:9 MSG

Savvy leaders understand the value of teamwork. They know that when teammates or coworkers learn the art of cooperation, everybody wins, but when cooperation breaks down, almost everybody in the organization suffers.

Are you a leader who emphasizes the importance of teamwork? Hopefully so, because in the world of sports or the world of business, cooperation pays and selfishness costs.

When everyone pulls in the same direction, mountains begin to move, but when it's "every man for himself," progress grinds to a halt. The happiest organizations are those in which everybody learns how to give and how to receive, with the emphasis on *give*.

If a team is to reach its potential, each player must be willing to subordinate his personal goals to the good of the team.
BUD WILKINSON

The only true satisfaction a player receives is the satisfaction that comes from being part of a successful team, regardless of his personal accomplishments.
VINCE LOMBARDI

It's amazing how much can be accomplished if no one cares who gets the credit.
JOHN WOODEN

Individual commitment to a group effort— that is what makes a team work, a company work, a society work, and a civilization work.
VINCE LOMBARDI

What is the recipe for successful achievement? Choose a career you love. Give it the best there is in you. Seize your opportunities. And be a member of the team.
BEN FRANKLIN

You've got to learn how to hold a team together. You lift some men up, calm others down, until finally they've got one heartbeat. Then, you've got yourself a team.
BEAR BRYANT

More from God's Word

Every kingdom divided against itself is headed for destruction,
and a house divided against itself falls.
LUKE 11:17 HCSB

Two people are better off than one,
for they can help each other succeed.
ECCLESIASTES 4:9 NLT

As iron sharpens iron, so people can improve each other.
PROVERBS 27:17 NCV

You must get along with each other. You must learn to be
considerate of one another, cultivating a life in common.
1 CORINTHIANS 1:10 MSG

A person standing alone can be attacked and defeated,
but two can stand back-to-back and conquer. Three are
even better, for a triple-braided cord is not easily broken.
ECCLESIASTES 4:12 NLT

A Timely Tip for Leaders

Leadership is not about titles, positions or flowcharts.
It is about one life influencing another.
JOHN MAXWELL

27

COURAGE

Be strong and courageous, and do the work.
Do not be afraid or discouraged,
for the LORD God, my God, is with you.
1 CHRONICLES 28:20 NIV

Christians have every reason to live—and to lead—courageously. After all, Jesus promises us that He has overcome the world and that He has made a place for us in heaven. But what about those short-term, everyday worries that keep us up at night? And what about the life-altering hardships that leave us wondering if we can ever recover? The answer, of course, is that because God cares for us in good times and hard times, we can turn our concerns over to Him in prayer, knowing that all things ultimately work for the good of those who love Him.

When you form a one-on-one relationship with your Creator, you can be comforted by the fact that wherever you find yourself, whether at the top of the mountain or the depths of the valley, God is there with you. And because your Creator cares for you and protects you, you can rise above your fears.

At this very moment the Lord is seeking to work in you and through you. He's asking you to live abundantly and courageously, and He's ready to help. So why not let Him do it . . . starting now?

Courage is not simply one of the virtues,
but the form of every virtue at the testing point.
C. S. LEWIS

Action springs not from thought,
but from a readiness for responsibility.
DIETRICH BONHOEFFER

Just as courage is faith in good, so discouragement
is faith in evil, and, while courage opens the door to good,
discouragement opens it to evil.
HANNAH WHITALL SMITH

In my experience, God rarely makes our fear disappear.
Instead, he asks us to be strong and take courage.
BRUCE WILKINSON

He who faces no calamity will need no courage.
Mysterious though it is, the characteristics
in human nature which we love best grow
in a soil with a strong mixture of troubles.
HARRY EMERSON FOSDICK

Courage is always the surest wisdom.
WINSTON CHURCHILL

More from God's Word

Be on guard. Stand firm in the faith.
Be courageous. Be strong.
1 Corinthians 16:13 NLT

For God has not given us a spirit of fearfulness,
but one of power, love, and sound judgment.
2 Timothy 1:7 HCSB

I can do all things through
Him who strengthens me.
Philippians 4:13 NASB

But He said to them,
"It is I; do not be afraid."
John 6:20 NKJV

Behold, God is my salvation;
I will trust, and not be afraid.
Isaiah 12:2 KJV

A Timely Tip for Leaders

Is your courage being tested today? If so, hold fast to God's promises and pray. God will give you the strength to meet any challenge if you ask Him sincerely and often. So ask.

28

COURTESY

Let everyone see that you are gentle and kind.
The Lord is coming soon.
PHILIPPIANS 4:5 NCV

God's Word makes is clear that we should treat others as we, ourselves, wish to be treated (Matthew 7:12). That means that we must be courteous to family, to friends, to acquaintances, to coworkers, and even to complete strangers.

Here in the twenty-first century, it sometimes seems like common courtesy is a decidedly uncommon trait. But if we are to trust the Bible—and we should—then we should understand that kindness and courtesy will never go out of style.

Today, as you fulfill your duties as a leader, try to be a little kinder than necessary to everyone you meet. And as you consider all the things God has done for you, honor Him with your good deeds and kind words. The Lord deserves no less, and neither, for that matter, do your loved ones.

There is a grace of kind listening,
as well as a grace of kind speaking.
FREDERICK W. FABER

You can motivate players better with
kind words than you can with a whip.
BUD WILKINSON

Praise loudly. Criticize softly.
LOU HOLTZ

The habit of being uniformly considerate toward others
will bring increased happiness to you.
GRENVILLE KLEISER

A man's manners are a mirror
in which he shows his portrait.
GOETHE

Good manners are nothing more
than the practical application of the Golden Rule.
LORETTA YOUNG

More from God's Word

*So, my friends, when you come together to the Lord's Table,
be reverent and courteous with one another.*
1 Corinthians 11:33 MSG

Do to others as you would have them do to you.
Luke 6:31 NIV

*Kind words are like honey—sweet to the soul
and healthy for the body.*
Proverbs 16:24 NLT

*Do not neglect to show hospitality to strangers, for by this
some have entertained angels without knowing it.*
Hebrews 13:2 NASB

*Finally, all of you be of one mind, having compassion for one
another; love as brothers, be tenderhearted, be courteous.*
1 Peter 3:8 NKJV

A Timely Tip for Leaders

If you're a Christian leader, courtesy isn't optional. If you disagree, do so without being disagreeable; if you're angry, hold your tongue; if you're frustrated or tired, don't argue. Instead, step away from the situation until you regain your composure.

29

CRITICISM

Do not judge others, and you will not be judged.
Do not condemn others, or it will all come back against you.
Forgive others, and you will be forgiven.
LUKE 6:37 NLT

Criticism comes in two flavors: constructive and destructive. Savvy leaders know the difference. They understand that a leader's role is to motivate, to encourage, to guide, and to set the right tone for the organization. The very best leaders understand that negativity breeds more negativity, so they find ways to deliver honest feedback without destroying their teammates' confidence.

You inhabit a world that's overflowing with negative messages, a world that, at times, seems dominated by pessimism, cynicism, doom, gloom, and very little else. Amid the sea of negativity and strife, it's easy to criticize, to complain, to moan, to groan, and to do very little else. But as a leader, you need a more constructive strategy.

So, the next time you're tempted to criticize or complain, ask yourself what you'd say if Jesus were looking over your shoulder. Because He is.

Sandwich every bit of criticism between
two heavy layers of praise.
MARY KAY ASH

The scrutiny we give other people
should be reserved for ourselves.
OSWALD CHAMBERS

Bear with the faults of others
as you would have them bear with yours.
PHILLIPS BROOKS

Discouraged people don't need critics.
They hurt enough already. What they need is encouragement.
They need a refuge, a willing, caring, available someone.
CHARLES SWINDOLL

Trust and thankfulness will get you safely through this day.
Trust protects you from worrying and obsessing.
Thankfulness keeps you from criticizing and complaining.
SARAH YOUNG

Those see nothing but faults who look for nothing else.
THOMAS FULLER

More from God's Word

Whoever derides their neighbor has no sense,
but the one who has understanding holds their tongue.
PROVERBS 11:12 NIV

Do everything without grumbling and arguing,
so that you may be blameless and pure.
PHILIPPIANS 2:14–15 HCSB

Those who guard their lips preserve their lives,
but those who speak rashly will come to ruin.
PROVERBS 13:3 NIV

LORD, set up a guard for my mouth;
keep watch at the door of my lips.
PSALM 141:3 HCSB

May these words of my mouth
and this meditation of my heart be pleasing in your sight,
Lord, my Rock and my Redeemer.
PSALM 19:14 NIV

A Timely Tip for Leaders

If you've acquired the habit of being overly critical—of others or yourself—it's time break the habit. Constant criticism is a poor way to motivate other people, and it's a poor way to motivate yourself.

30
DECISIONS

But if any of you needs wisdom, you should ask God for it.
He is generous to everyone and will give you
wisdom without criticizing you.

JAMES 1:5 NCV

Leaders must make decisions, and the quality of those decisions will determine the success or failure of the endeavor. Good leaders make good decisions. Poor leaders make poor decisions. And great leaders make great decisions.

The Bible offers clear guidance about decision making. So if you're about to make an important decision, here are some things you can do: 1. Gather information. Don't expect to get all the facts—that's impossible—but try to gather as much information as you can in a reasonable amount of time (Proverbs 24:3–4). 2. Be patient: If you have time to make a decision, use that time to make a good decision (Proverbs 19:2). 3. Rely on the counsel of a few friends and mentors. Proverbs 1:5 makes it clear: "A wise man will hear and increase learning, and a man of understanding will attain wise counsel." (NKJV). 4. Pray for guidance and listen carefully to your conscience. 5. When the time for action arrives, act. Procrastination is the enemy of progress; don't let it defeat you (James 1:22).

*Once God leads you to make a decision, don't draw back.
Instead, trust His leading and believe He goes before you—
because He does.*

BILLY GRAHAM

*A man who honors God privately will
show it by making good decisions publically.*

EDWIN LOUIS COLE

*Every day, I find countless opportunities to decide whether I
will obey God and demonstrate my love for Him or try to please
myself or the world system. God is waiting for my choices.*

BILL BRIGHT

Get into the habit of dealing with God about everything.

OSWALD CHAMBERS

*Our battles are first won or lost in the secret places of our will
in God's presence, never in full view of the world.*

OSWALD CHAMBERS

*Men are free to decide their own moral choices, but they are
also under the necessity to account to God for those choices.*

A. W. TOZIER

More from God's Word

In every way be an example of doing good deeds.
When you teach, do it with honesty and seriousness.
TITUS 2:7 NCV

We can make our own plans, but the LORD
gives the right answer. People may be pure in their own eyes,
but the LORD examines their motives.
PROVERBS 16:1–2 NLT

Blessed is the man who walks
not in the counsel of the ungodly, nor stands in the
path of sinners, nor sits in the seat of the scornful.
PSALM 1:1 NKJV

The highway of the upright avoids evil;
the one who guards his way protects his life.
PROVERBS 16:17 HCSB

By their fruits ye shall know them.
MATTHEW 7:20 KJV

A Timely Tip for Leaders

Every step of your life's journey is a choice, and the overall quality of your decisions will help determine the overall quality of the journey. To make better choices, listen carefully to your conscience, trust God's Word, and follow as closely as you can in the footsteps of His Son.

31

DEVOTIONALS AND QUIET TIME

Morning by morning he wakens me and opens my understanding to his will. The Sovereign LORD has spoken to me, and I have listened.

ISAIAH 50:4–5 NLT

Even the wisest leaders can't be successful by themselves. They need mentors; they need advisors; but, most of all, they need God. And, if you want to maximize your leadership skills, you'll begin your day with the ultimate Counselor: your Father in heaven.

Every day of your life has 1,440 minutes, and God deserves a few of them. And, you deserve the experience of spending a few quiet minutes every morning with your Creator. So, if you haven't already done so, establish the habit of spending time with God every day of the week. It's a habit that will change your day and revolutionize your life. When you give the Lord your undivided attention, everything changes, including you.

*Make it the first morning business of your life
to understand some part of the Bible clearly,
and make it your daily business to obey it.*
JOHN RUSKIN

*Make the Bible part of your daily life,
and ask God to engrave its truths on your soul.*
BILLY GRAHAM

*Whatever is your best time in the day,
give that to communion with God.*
HUDSON TAYLOR

*Relying on God has to begin all over again
every day as if nothing had yet been done.*
C. S. LEWIS

Prayer-time must be kept up as duly as meal-time.
MATTHEW HENRY

*The entire day receives order and discipline when it acquires
unity. This unity must be sought and found in morning prayer.
The morning prayer determines the day.*
DIETRICH BONHOEFFER

More from God's Word

It is good to give thanks to the LORD,
And to sing praises to Your name, O Most High.
PSALM 92:1 NKJV

Heaven and earth will pass away,
but My words will never pass away.
MATTHEW 24:35 HCSB

Thy word is a lamp unto my feet, and a light unto my path.
PSALM 119:105 KJV

Early the next morning, while it was still dark, Jesus woke and
left the house. He went to a lonely place, where he prayed.
MARK 1:35 NCV

But grow in the grace and knowledge
of our Lord and Savior Jesus Christ. To Him be the glory
both now and to the day of eternity.
2 PETER 3:18 HCSB

A Timely Tip for Leaders

As a Christian leader, you need a regular appointment with
your Creator. A regular time of quiet reflection and prayer will
allow you to praise your Creator, to focus your thoughts, and to
seek God's guidance on matters great and small. Don't miss this
opportunity.

32

DISAPPOINTMENTS

Then they cried out to the LORD in their trouble,
and He saved them out of their distresses.
PSALM 107:13 NKJV

As we make the journey from the cradle to the grave, disappointments are inevitable. No matter how competent we are, no matter how fortunate, we still encounter circumstances that fall far short of our expectations. When tough times arrive, we have choices to make: We can feel sorry for ourselves or we can get angry or we can become depressed. Or, we can get busy praying about out problems and solving them.

When we are disheartened—on those cloudy days when our strength is sapped and our hope is shaken—there exists a source from which we can draw perspective and courage. That source is God. When we turn everything over to Him, we find that He is sufficient to meet our needs. No problem is too big for Him.

So, the next time you feel disappointed, slow down long enough to have a serious talk with your Creator. Pray for guidance, pray for strength, and pray for the wisdom to trust your heavenly Father. Your disappointments are temporary; His love is not.

Unless we learn to deal with disappointment,
it will rob us of joy and poison our souls.
BILLY GRAHAM

If your hopes are being disappointed just now,
it means that they are being purified.
OSWALD CHAMBERS

Discouragement is the opposite of faith.
It is Satan's device to thwart the work of God in your life.
BILLY GRAHAM

Everyone gets discouraged. The question is:
Are you going to give up or get up? It's a choice.
JOHN MAXWELL

If I had permitted my failures to discourage me, I cannot see
any way in which I would ever have made progress.
CALVIN COOLIDGE

Never flinch; never weary; never despair.
WINSTON CHURCHILL

MORE FROM GOD'S WORD

He heals the brokenhearted and binds up their wounds.
PSALM 147:3 HCSB

He shall not be afraid of evil tidings:
his heart is fixed, trusting in the LORD.
PSALM 112:7 KJV

Many adversities come to the one who is righteous,
but the LORD delivers him from them all.
PSALM 34:19 HCSB

My son, do not despise the chastening of the LORD,
nor be discouraged when you are rebuked by Him.
HEBREWS 12:5 NKJV

They that sow in tears shall reap in joy.
PSALM 126:5 KJV

A TIMELY TIP FOR LEADERS

When you're disappointed or hurt don't spend too much time asking, "Why me, Lord?" Instead, ask, "What now, Lord?" and then get busy. When you do, you'll feel much better.

33

DISCIPLINE

Discipline yourself for the purpose of godliness.
1 TIMOTHY 4:7 NASB

The best leaders understand the importance of discipline: for their followers *and* for themselves. It's not enough to preach the fine art of discipline; we must also live disciplined lives. Otherwise, our actions speak so loudly that our words become meaningless.

God does not reward apathy, laziness, or idleness, nor does He reward undisciplined behavior. Our heavenly Father has a way of helping those who first help themselves, and He expects us to lead disciplined lives despite worldly temptations to do otherwise.

The media glorifies leisure. The ultimate goal, so the message goes, is to win the lottery and then retire to some sunny paradise in order to while away the hours sitting idly by watching the waves splash onto the sand. Such leisure activities are fine for a few days, but not for a lifetime.

Life's greatest rewards are seldom the result of luck. More often than not, our greatest accomplishments require plenty of discipline and lots of work, which is perfectly fine with God. After all, He knows that we can do the work, and He knows the rewards that we'll earn when we finish the job. Besides, God knows that He will always help us complete the tasks He has set before us. As a matter of fact, God usually does at least half the work: the *second* half.

*In reading the lives of great men, I found
that the first victory they won was over themselves:
with all of them, self-discipline came first.*
HARRY S TRUMAN

*Pray as though everything depended on God.
Work as though everything depended on you.*
ST. AUGUSTINE

*The best preparation for the future is the
present well seen to, and the last duty done.*
GEORGE MACDONALD

*I've never known a really successful man who deep in his heart
did not understand the grind, the discipline it takes to win.*
VINCE LOMBARDI

*Think of something you ought to do and go do it.
Heed not your feelings. Do your work.*
GEORGE MACDONALD

Discipline yourself and others won't have to.
JOHN WOODEN

MORE FROM GOD'S WORD

Whatever you do, do your work heartily,
as for the Lord rather than for men.
COLOSSIANS 3:23 NASB

Better to be patient than powerful;
better to have self-control than to conquer a city.
PROVERBS 16:32 NLT

But the fruit of the Spirit is love, joy, peace, patience,
kindness, goodness, faith, gentleness, self-control.
Against such things there is no law.
GALATIANS 5:22–23 HCSB

Finishing is better than starting.
Patience is better than pride.
ECCLESIASTES 7:8 NLT

A final word: Be strong in the Lord
and in his mighty power.
EPHESIANS 6:10 NLT

A TIMELY TIP FOR LEADERS

In reading the lives of great men, I found
that the first victory they won was over themselves:
with all of them, self-discipline came first.
HARRY S TRUMAN

34

DISCOURAGEMENT

Give your burdens to the Lord, and he will take care of you.
He will not permit the godly to slip and fall.
PSALM 55:22 NLT

Even the most optimistic Christians may, from time to time, become discouraged. After all, we live in a demanding world where expectations are high and stressors are ubiquitous. When we face the inevitable burdens and discouragements of life here on Earth, we may be tempted to abandon hope. But God has other plans. The Lord knows exactly how He intends to use us. Our task is to remain faithful until He does.

On those cloudy days when worries threaten to overwhelm us, we can turn to our heavenly Father for courage and assurance. When we do, the Lord offers guidance and strength.

As a follower of Christ, you have every reason to be hopeful. So, if you have become discouraged by the direction of your day or your life, take a few quiet moments and redirect your thoughts to the Lord and His blessings. Your heavenly Father is a God of possibility, not negativity. He is your shepherd, and the ultimate victory will most certainly be His. God's promise is made clear in Isaiah 40:31: "But those who wait on the LORD shall renew their strength; they shall mount up with wings like eagles, they shall run and not be weary, they shall walk and not faint" (NKJV). And upon this promise you can—and should—depend.

Everyone gets discouraged. The question is:
Are you going to give up or get up? It's a choice.
JOHN MAXWELL

Discouragement is the opposite of faith.
It is Satan's device to thwart the work of God in your life.
BILLY GRAHAM

We never get anywhere—nor do our conditions and
circumstances change—when we look at the dark side of life.
LETTIE COWMAN

Thanksgiving or complaining—these words express two
contrasting attitudes of the souls of God's children. The soul
that gives thanks can find comfort in everything; the soul that
complains can find comfort in nothing.
HANNAH WHITALL SMITH

The great paralysis of our heart is unbelief.
OSWALD CHAMBERS

Thinking of and serving with others can be an antidote to
negative and unhealthy introspection.
BILLY GRAHAM

MORE FROM GOD'S WORD

The LORD is a refuge for His people and a stronghold.
JOEL 3:16 NASB

The LORD is near to those who have a broken heart.
PSALM 34:18 NKJV

God shall wipe away all the tears from their eyes.
REVELATION 7:17 KJV

If God is for us, who is against us?
ROMANS 8:31 HCSB

*God is our refuge and strength,
a very present help in trouble.*
PSALM 46:1 NKJV

A TIMELY TIP FOR LEADERS

If you genuinely believe that God is good and that His Son died for your sins, how can you be pessimistic about your future? The answer, of course, is that you can't!

35

DREAMS

When dreams come true, there is life and joy.
PROVERBS 13:12 NLT

How big are your dreams? Are you expecting God to help you move mountains, or have you succumbed to pessimism and doubt? The answer to these questions will, to a surprising extent, determine the quality of your day and the direction of your life.

God has big plans for you, and He has equipped you with everything you need to make His plans come true. When the dream in your heart is one that God has placed there, miracles happen. Your challenge, of course, is to make certain that God's plans and your dreams coincide.

So keep believing in yourself, keep talking to your Creator, and keep working. And, don't be afraid to dream big. After all, with God as your partner, there's no limit to the things that the two of you, working together, can accomplish.

If you can dream it, then you can achieve it.
You will get all you want in life if you
help enough other people get what they want.
ZIG ZIGLAR

Perhaps the greatest psychological, spiritual, and medical need
that all people have is the need for hope.
BILLY GRAHAM

A dream doesn't become reality through magic;
it takes sweat, determination and hard work.
COLIN POWELL

Dreams never hurt anybody who kept working right behind
the dream to make as much of it come true as possible.
F. W. WOOLWORTH

Two types of voices command your attention today.
Negative ones fill your mind with doubt, bitterness,
and fear. Positive ones purvey hope and strength.
Which one will you choose to heed?
MAX LUCADO

Our prospects are as bright as the promises of God.
ADRONIUM JUDSON

More from God's Word

Hope deferred makes the heart sick.
PROVERBS 13:12 NKJV

Where there is no vision, the people perish.
PROVERBS 29:18 KJV

*But we are hoping for something we do not have yet,
and we are waiting for it patiently.*
ROMANS 8:25 NCV

*Now may the God of hope fill you with all joy
and peace as you believe in Him so that you may
overflow with hope by the power of the Holy Spirit.*
ROMANS 15:13 HCSB

*Humble yourselves therefore under the mighty hand of God,
that he may exalt you in due time.*
1 PETER 5:6 KJV

A Timely Tip for Leaders

You can dream big dreams, but you can never out-dream God. His plans for you are even bigger than you can imagine. Entrust your future to Him.

36

ENCOURAGEMENT

But encourage each other daily, while it is still called today,
so that none of you is hardened by sin's deception.
HEBREWS 3:13 HCSB

As a Christian leader, you have every reason to be hopeful, enthusiastic, and optimistic. And you have every reason to share your positive expectations with others. When you do, you'll discover that optimism, like other human emotions, is contagious.

As a follower of the One from Galilee, you have the opportunity to become a beacon of encouragement to the world. How can you do it? By looking for the good in others and celebrating the good that you find. As the old saying goes, "When someone does something good, applaud. You'll make two people happy!"

Even a brief word of appreciation can make a big difference in someone's life. So how many people will you encourage today? Ten? Twenty? Even more than that? The answer you give will help determine the quality of *their* lives *and* the quality of *yours*.

*When we are the comfort and
encouragement to others, we are sometimes surprised at
how it comes back to us many times over.*
BILLY GRAHAM

*Discouraged people don't need critics. They hurt enough
already. What they need is encouragement. They need a refuge,
a willing, caring, available someone.*
CHARLES SWINDOLL

*All around you are people whose lives are
filled with trouble and sorrow.
They need your compassion and encouragement.*
BILLY GRAHAM

*Encouragement is awesome. It can actually
change the course of another person's day, week, or life.*
CHARLES SWINDOLL

*I will speak ill of no man and speak
all the good I know of everybody.*
BEN FRANKLIN

*Correction does much, but encouragement does more.
Encouragement after censure is as the sun after a shower.*
GOETHE

More from God's Word

*Let us think about each other and help each other
to show love and do good deeds.*
HEBREWS 10:24 NCV

Bear one another's burdens, and so fulfill the law of Christ.
GALATIANS 6:2 NKJV

*So encourage each other and give each other strength,
just as you are doing now.*
1 THESSALONIANS 5:11 NCV

*When you talk, do not say harmful things, but say
what people need—words that will help others become stronger.
Then what you say will do good to those who listen to you.*
EPHESIANS 4:29 NCV

*Now we exhort you, brethren, warn those who are unruly,
comfort the fainthearted, uphold the weak, be patient with all.*
1 THESSALONIANS 5:14 NKJV

A Timely Tip for Leaders

When you help other people feel better about themselves, you'll
feel better about yourself, too. So what are you waiting for?

37

ENTHUSIASM

Whatever you do, do it enthusiastically,
as something done for the Lord and not for men.
COLOSSIANS 3:23 HCSB

As a Christian leader, you have many reasons to be enthusiastic about your life, your opportunities, your team, and your future. After all, your eternal destiny is secure. Christ died for your sins, and He wants you to experience life abundant and life eternal. So what's not to get excited about?

Are you an enthusiastic leader and a passionate Christian? Are you genuinely excited about your faith, your career, and your future? Hopefully, you can answer these questions with a resounding yes. But if your passion for the tasks of life has waned, it's time to slow down long enough to recharge your spiritual batteries, to reflect on your plans, and then reorder your priorities.

Each new day is an opportunity to put God first and celebrate His creation. Today, take time to count your blessings and take stock of your opportunities. And while you're at it, ask God for strength. When you sincerely petition Him, He will give you everything you need to live well and lead well.

We act as though comfort and luxury were the chief
requirements of life, when all that we need to make us really
happy is something to be enthusiastic about.
CHARLES KINGSLEY

Wherever you are, be all there. Live to the hilt
every situation you believe to be the will of God.
JIM ELLIOT

Those who have achieved excellence in the
practice of an art or profession have commonly been
motivated by great enthusiasm in their pursuit of it.
JOHN KNOX

Instead of living a black-and-white existence, we'll be released
into a Technicolor world of vibrancy and emotion when we
more accurately reflect His nature to the world around us.
BILL HYBELS

Two types of voices command your attention today.
Negative ones fill your mind with doubt, bitterness,
and fear. Positive ones purvey hope and strength.
Which one will you choose to heed?
MAX LUCADO

Energy and persistence alter all things.
BEN FRANKLIN

MORE FROM GOD'S WORD

Do your work with enthusiasm. Work as if you were serving the Lord, not as if you were serving only men and women.
EPHESIANS 6:7 NCV

A happy heart makes the face cheerful,
but heartache crushes the spirit.
PROVERBS 15:13 NIV

But as for me, I will hope continually,
and will praise You yet more and more.
PSALM 71:14 NASB

Rejoice always! Pray constantly. Give thanks in everything,
for this is God's will for you in Christ Jesus.
1 THESSALONIANS 5:16–18 HCSB

Let the hearts of those who seek the LORD rejoice.
Look to the LORD and his strength; seek his face always.
1 CHRONICLES 16:10–11 NIV

A TIMELY TIP FOR LEADERS

Today, as you interact with family, friends, and coworkers, share your courage, your hopes, your dreams, and your enthusiasm. Your positive outlook will be almost as big a blessing to them as it is to you.

38

EXAMPLE

You should be an example to the believers
in speech, in conduct, in love, in faith, in purity.
1 TIMOTHY 4:12 HCSB

All of us are role models. Whether we like it or not, our actions speak volumes—much more loudly, in fact, than our words—to friends, to family members, to coworkers, and to teammates. What kind of example are you? Are your actions encouraging others to follow in the footsteps of God's Son? Hopefully so.

You live in a dangerous, distraction-filled world, brimming with temptations. That's why you encounter so many opportunities to stray from God's path. Your task, of course, is to avoid the distractions and reject the temptations. When you do, you'll serve as a powerful example and a positive role model in a world that desperately needs both.

Our walk counts far more than our talk, always!
GEORGE MUELLER

People are watching the way we act
more than they are listening to what we say.
MAX LUCADO

Be such a man, and live such a life,
that if every man were such as you, and every life
a life like yours, this earth would be God's Paradise.
PHILLIPS BROOKS

Be a good witness by the way you live. The way we live
is often more convincing than the words we say.
BILLY GRAHAM

Those who teach by their doctrine must teach by their life,
or else they pull down with one hand
what they build up with the other.
MATTHEW HENRY

If you want to teach, be a role model.
That's the most powerful form of teaching
JOHN WOODEN

More from God's Word

*For you were once darkness, but now you are
light in the Lord. Walk as children of light—for the fruit of
the light results in all goodness, righteousness, and truth—
discerning what is pleasing to the Lord.*
EPHESIANS 5:8–10 HCSB

If we live in the Spirit, let us also walk in the Spirit.
GALATIANS 5:25 NKJV

*Who among you is wise and understanding? Let him show
by his good behavior his deeds in the gentleness of wisdom.*
JAMES 3:13 NASB

*But prove yourselves doers of the word,
and not merely hearers who delude themselves.*
JAMES 1:22 NASB

*In any case, we should live up to
whatever truth we have attained.*
PHILIPPIANS 3:16:HCSB

A Timely Tip for Leaders

As a Christian leader, the most important light you shine is the
light that your own life shines on the lives of others. May your
light shine brightly, obediently, and eternally.

39

EXCELLENCE

Whatever you do, work at it with all your heart,
as working for the Lord, not for men.
COLOSSIANS 3:23 NIV

The legendary football coach Vince Lombardi observed, "The quality of a person's life is in direct proportion to his commitment to excellence, regardless of his chosen field of endeavor." Wise leaders agree. The rewards of excellence are many; the rewards of mediocrity are few.

The Lord has created a world in which quality work is rewarded and sloppy work is not. Yet sometimes, we're tempted to seek ease over excellence. Or we may—mistakenly—search for shortcuts when God intends that we take a different, more rigorous path.

So, wherever you find yourself, whether you're leading a Fortune 500 company or building a startup business in your garage, strive for excellence. Strive for quality solutions, not quick-and-easy fixes. When you do, your work will be rewarded and God find a way to bless your efforts. Simply do your best with determination and purpose, and leave the rest up to Him.

It is our best work that God wants,
not the dregs of our exhaustion.
I think he must prefer quality to quantity.
GEORGE MACDONALD

The secret of living a life of excellence is merely a
matter of thinking thoughts of excellence. Really,
it's a matter of programming our minds with the kind of
information that will set us free.
CHARLES SWINDOLL

The difference between something good
and something great is attention to detail.
CHARLES SWINDOLL

The quest for excellence is a mark of maturity.
The quest for power is childish.
MAX LUCADO

When love and skill work together,
expect a masterpiece.
JOHN RUSKIN

Never confuse activity with productivity.
RICK WARREN

More from God's Word

But as for you, be strong; don't be discouraged,
for your work has a reward.
2 CHRONICLES 15:7 HCSB

Do not lack diligence; be fervent in spirit; serve the Lord.
ROMANS 12:11 HCSB

Don't work only while being watched,
in order to please men, but as slaves of Christ,
do God's will from your heart. Serve with
a good attitude as to the Lord and not to men.
EPHESIANS 6:6–7 HCSB

Be strong and courageous, and do the work.
Don't be afraid or discouraged, for the LORD God, my God,
is with you. He will not fail you or forsake you.
1 CHRONICLES 28:20 NLT

He did it with all his heart. So he prospered.
2 CHRONICLES 31:21 NKJV

A Timely Tip for Leaders

Excellence is habit forming, so give your best every time you go
to work. As your talents increase, so will your responsibilities and
your rewards.

40

FAILURE

For though the righteous fall seven times, they rise again.
PROVERBS 24:16 NIV

Occasional mistakes, setbacks, disappointments, and failures are the price that we must pay for taking risks and trying new things. Even the best-intentioned plans sometimes go astray, and when they do, we must never lose faith. When we fail, we must not label ourselves as "failures." Instead, we should pick ourselves up, dust ourselves off, learn from our mistakes, and reengage with life.

Have you encountered a recent setback? If so, what did you learn? And, how can you apply your hard-earned wisdom to the challenges that are ahead of you?

If you've experienced a recent failure, remember that God still has big plans for your life. And, while you're waiting for those plans to unfold, keep working, keep praying, and keep the faith. The Lord can build a road through any wilderness. Even yours.

In God's economy nothing is wasted.
Through failure, we learn a lesson in humility which is
probably needed, painful though it is.
BILL WILSON

No matter how badly we have failed,
we can always get up and begin again.
Our God is the God of new beginnings.
WARREN WIERSBE

Mistakes offer the possibility for redemption and a
new start in God's kingdom. No matter what you're guilty of,
God can restore your innocence.
BARBARA JOHNSON

No amount of falls will really undo us if we keep picking
ourselves up after each one.
C. S. LEWIS

Those who have failed miserably are often
the first to see God's formula for success.
ERWIN LUTZER

Goals are worth setting and worth missing.
We learn from non-successes.
BILL BRIGHT

More from God's Word

The LORD is near to those who have a broken heart.
PSALM 34:18 NKJV

*If you listen to correction to improve your life,
you will live among the wise.*
PROVERBS 15:31 NCV

*We are hard-pressed on every side, yet not crushed;
we are perplexed, but not in despair.*
2 CORINTHIANS 4:8 NKJV

*But as for you, be strong; don't be discouraged,
for your work has a reward.*
2 CHRONICLES 15:7 HCSB

*Weeping may endure for a night,
but joy cometh in the morning.*
PSALM 30:5 KJV

A Timely Tip for Leaders

Failures are inevitable—your response to them is optional. You can always find a way to turn a stumbling block into a stepping stone . . . and you should.

41

FAITH

For truly I say to you, if you have faith the size of a mustard seed, you will say to this mountain, "Move from here to there," and it will move; and nothing will be impossible to you.
MATTHEW 17:20 NASB

The Bible makes it clear—and Christian leaders understand—that faith is powerful. With it, we can move mountains. With it, we can endure any hardship. With it, we can rise above the challenges of everyday life and live victoriously, whatever our circumstances.

Is your faith strong enough to move the mountains in your own life? If so, you're already tapped in to a source of strength that never fails: God's strength. But if your spiritual batteries are in need of recharging, don't be discouraged. God's strength is always available to those who seek.

The first element of a successful life is faith: faith in God, faith in His promises, and faith in His Son. When our faith in the Creator is strong, we can then have faith in ourselves, knowing that we are tools in the hands of a loving God who made mountains—and moves them—according to a perfect plan that only He can see.

Faith points us beyond our problems
to the hope we have in Christ.
BILLY GRAHAM

Fear imprisons, faith liberates; fear paralyzes, faith empowers;
fear disheartens, faith encourages; fear sickens, faith heals;
fear makes useless, faith makes serviceable.
HARRY EMERSON FOSDICK

Shout the shout of faith. Nothing can withstand the
triumphant faith that links itself to omnipotence.
The secret of all successful living lies in this shout of faith.
HANNAH WHITALL SMITH

I have learned that faith means trusting in advance
what will only make sense in reverse.
PHILLIP YANCEY

Faith does not concern itself with the entire journey.
One step is enough.
LETTIE COWMAN

Faith is not merely holding on to God.
It is God holding on to you.
CORRIE TEN BOOM

More from God's Word

Don't be afraid, because I am your God.
I will make you strong and will help you; I will support you
with my right hand that saves you.
ISAIAH 41:10 NCV

Don't be afraid. Only believe.
MARK 5:36 HCSB

Blessed are they that have not seen,
and yet have believed.
JOHN 20:29 KJV

All things are possible for the one who believes.
MARK 9:23 NCV

And he said unto her, Daughter, thy faith hath made thee
whole; go in peace, and be whole.
MARK 5:34 KJV

A Timely Tip for Leaders

If your faith is strong enough, you and God—working together—
can move mountains. No challenge is too big for God.

42

FEAR AND THE FEAR OF FAILURE

*Peace I leave with you; My peace I give to you;
not as the world gives do I give to you. Do not
let your heart be troubled, nor let it be fearful.*

JOHN 14:27 NASB

All leaders experience difficult days when unexpected circumstances test their mettle. Difficult times call for courageous measures. Running away from problems only perpetuates them; fear begets more fear; and, anxiety is a poor counselor. As John Maxwell observed, "People who focus on their fears don't grow. They become paralyzed."

Adversity visits everyone—no human being is beyond Old Man Trouble's reach. But, Old Man Trouble is not only an unwelcome guest, he is also an invaluable teacher. If we are to become mature human beings, it is our duty to learn from the inevitable hardships and disappointments of life.

Today, ask God to help you step beyond the boundaries of your fear. Ask Him to guide you to a place where you can realize your potential and help others reach theirs. Ask Him to do His part, and then promise Him that you'll do your part. Don't ask God to lead you to a safe place; ask Him to lead you to the right place. And remember that those two places are seldom the same.

The presence of fear does not mean you have no faith.
Fear visits everyone. But make
your fear a visitor and not a resident.
MAX LUCADO

It is good to remind ourselves that the will of God comes from
the heart of God and that we need not be afraid.
WARREN WIERSBE

A perfect faith would lift us absolutely above fear.
GEORGE MACDONALD

The Lord Jesus by His Holy Spirit is with me,
and the knowledge of His presence
dispels the darkness and allays any fears.
BILL BRIGHT

The presence of hope in the invincible
sovereignty of God drives out fear.
JOHN PIPER

Meet your fears with faith.
MAX LUCADO

MORE FROM GOD'S WORD

But He said to them, "It is I; do not be afraid."
JOHN 6:20 NKJV

*Fear not, for I am with you; be not dismayed, for I
am your God. I will strengthen you, yes, I will help you,
I will uphold you with My righteous right hand.*
ISAIAH 41:10 NKJV

*The LORD is my light and my salvation—
whom should I fear? The LORD is the stronghold of my life—
of whom should I be afraid?*
PSALM 27:1 HCSB

*Even though I walk through the darkest valley,
I will fear no evil, for you are with me;
your rod and your staff, they comfort me.*
PSALM 23:4 NIV

Be not afraid, only believe.
MARK 5:36 KJV

A TIMELY TIP FOR LEADERS

Are you feeling anxious or fearful? If so, trust God to handle those
problems that are simply too big for you to solve. Entrust the
future—your future—to God.

43

FOLLOWING CHRIST

Then He said to them all, "If anyone
wants to come with Me, he must deny himself,
take up his cross daily, and follow Me."
LUKE 9:23 HCSB

Every day, we're presented with countless opportunities to honor God by following in the footsteps of His Son. But we're sorely tempted to do otherwise. The world is filled to the brim with temptations and distractions that beckon us down a different path.

Bill Bright observed, "We must always invite Jesus to be the navigator of our plans, desires, wills, and emotions, for He is the way, the truth, and the life."

Today, don't just be a leader. Be a follower, too: a follower of the One from Galilee. Do your part to take up the cross and follow Him, even if the world encourages you to do otherwise. When you're traveling step-by-step with the Son of God, you're always on the right path.

To be a disciple of Jesus means to learn from Him,
to follow Him. The cost may be high.
BILLY GRAHAM

A disciple is a follower of Christ. That means
you take on His priorities as your own. His agenda
becomes your agenda. His mission becomes your mission.
CHARLES STANLEY

Christ is not valued at all unless He is valued above all.
ST. AUGUSTINE

Be assured, if you walk with Him and look to Him,
and expect help from Him, He will never fail you.
GEORGE MUELLER

As you walk through the valley of the unknown, you will find
the footprints of Jesus both in front of you and beside you.
CHARLES STANLEY

The beautiful thing about this adventure called faith is that
we can count on Him never to lead us astray.
CHARLES SWINDOLL

More from God's Word

But whoever keeps His word, truly in him the love of God is perfected. This is how we know we are in Him: The one who says he remains in Him should walk just as He walked.
1 John 2:5–6 HCSB

Walk in a manner worthy of the God who calls you into His own kingdom and glory.
1 Thessalonians 2:12 NASB

For we walk by faith, not by sight.
2 Corinthians 5:7 HCSB

Take my yoke upon you, and learn of me; for I am meek and lowly in heart: and ye shall find rest unto your souls. For my yoke is easy, and my burden is light.
Matthew 11:29–30 KJV

Whoever is not willing to carry the cross and follow me is not worthy of me. Those who try to hold on to their lives will give up true life. Those who give up their lives for me will hold on to true life.
Matthew 10:38–39 NCV

A Timely Tip for Leaders

Think about your relationship with Jesus: what it is, and what it can be. Then, as you embark upon the next phase of your leadership journey, be sure to walk with your Savior every step of the way.

44

FORGIVENESS

Judge not, and you shall not be judged.
Condemn not, and you shall not be condemned.
Forgive, and you will be forgiven.
LUKE 6:37 NKJV

Forgiveness is a gift of great value, but ironically it's a gift that is often worth more to the giver than to the recipient. You simply cannot give the gift of forgiveness without receiving an important blessing for yourself.

From a psychological perspective, the act of forgiving relieves you of some very heavy mental baggage: persistent feelings of hatred, anger, and regret. More importantly, the act of forgiveness brings with it a spiritual blessing, a knowledge that you have honored your heavenly Father by obeying His commandments.

Simply put, forgiveness is a gift that you give yourself by giving it to someone else. When you make the choice to forgive, everybody wins, including you.

Forgiveness does not change the past,
but it does enlarge the future.
DAVID JEREMIAH

Bitterness imprisons life; love releases it.
HARRY EMERSON FOSDICK

Forgiveness is one of the most beautiful words in the
human vocabulary. How much pain could be avoided
if we all learned the meaning of this word!
BILLY GRAHAM

In one bold stroke, forgiveness obliterates the past
and permits us to enter the land of new beginnings.
BILLY GRAHAM

Forgiveness is an act of the will, and the will can function
regardless of the temperature of the heart.
CORRIE TEN BOOM

Forgiveness is God's command.
MARTIN LUTHER

More from God's Word

Above all, love each other deeply, because
love covers a multitude of sins.
1 Peter 4:8 NIV

But I say to you, love your enemies
and pray for those who persecute you.
Matthew 5:44 NASB

And be kind to one another, tenderhearted, forgiving
one another, even as God in Christ forgave you.
Ephesians 4:32 NKJV

And whenever you stand praying, if you have anything
against anyone, forgive him, so that your Father in heaven
will also forgive you your wrongdoing.
Mark 11:25 HCSB

The merciful are blessed,
for they will be shown mercy.
Matthew 5:7 HCSB

A Timely Tip for Leaders

Forgiveness is its own reward. Bitterness is its own punishment. Guard your words and thoughts accordingly.

45

GIFTS

Do not neglect the gift that is in you.
1 TIMOTHY 4:14 NKJV

God gives each of us special talents and opportunities. And He bestows these gifts for a reason: so that we might use them for His glory. But the world tempts us to do otherwise. Here in the twenty-first century, life is filled to the brim with distractions and temptations, each of which has the potential to distance us from the path God intends us to take.

Do you possess financial resources? Share them. Do you have a spiritual gift? Share it. Do you have a personal testimony about the things that Christ has done for you? Tell your story. Do you possess a particular talent? Hone that skill and use it for God's glory.

All your talents, all your opportunities, and all your gifts are on temporary loan from the Creator. Use those gifts while you can because time is short and the needs are great. In every undertaking, make God your partner. Then, just as He promised, God will bless you now and forever.

You weren't an accident. You weren't mass produced.
You aren't an assembly-line product. You were
deliberately planned, specifically gifted, and lovingly
positioned on the Earth by the Master Craftsman.

MAX LUCADO

Our purpose should be to discover the gifts He has given us and
to use those gifts faithfully and joyfully in His service, without
either envying or disparaging the gifts we do not have.

JOHN MACARTHUR

God has given you special talents—
now it's your turn to give them back to God.

MARIE T. FREEMAN

If others don't use their gifts, you get cheated,
and if you don't use your gifts, they get cheated.

RICK WARREN

Talent is God-given; be humble. Fame is man-given;
be thankful. Conceit is self-given; be careful.

JOHN WOODEN

At the end of your life on earth you will be
evaluated and rewarded according to how well you
handled what God entrusted to you.

RICK WARREN

More from God's Word

*God has given each of you a gift from his great variety
of spiritual gifts. Use them well to serve one another.*
1 PETER 4:10 NLT

Now there are diversities of gifts, but the same Spirit.
1 CORINTHIANS 12:4 KJV

*Every good and perfect gift is from above,
coming down from the Father of the heavenly lights,
who does not change like shifting shadows.*
JAMES 1:17 NIV

*His master replied, "Well done, good and faithful servant!
You have been faithful with a few things;
I will put you in charge of many things.
Come and share your master's happiness!"*
MATTHEW 25:21 NIV

I remind you to fan into flame the gift of God.
2 TIMOTHY 1:6 NIV

A Timely Tip for Leaders

God has given you a unique array of talents and opportunities. If
you use your gifts wisely, they're multiplied. If you misuse your
gifts—or ignore them altogether—they are lost. God is anxious for
you to use your gifts . . . are you?

46
GOALS

But a noble person plans noble things;
he stands up for noble causes.
ISAIAH 32:8 HCSB

As a Christian leader, are you determined to set worthy goals? And will you encourage the people you lead to do likewise? Hopefully, you'll answer these two questions with a resounding yes.

God has a noble plan for your life, an important plan, a plan that only you can fulfill. But there's a catch: You live in a world that entices you to squander your resources and your time in a real-life game of Trivial Pursuit. The temptation to pursue trivialities is a temptation you should avoid.

Instead of focusing on the inevitable distractions and temptations of everyday life, you must strive to make worthy plans and set worthy goals. Then, you must summon the courage and determination to turn those goals into reality. Don't settle for second-best, and don't sell yourself short. Even if your goals seem to stretch you to the limit, don't be discouraged. There's no limit to the things that you and God—working together—can accomplish.

*The discipline to prioritize and the ability to work toward a
stated goal are essential to a leader's success.*
JOHN MAXWELL

*It is important to set goals because if you do not have a plan,
a goal, a direction, a purpose, and a focus, you are not
going to accomplish anything for the glory of God.*
BILL BRIGHT

*Set goals so big that unless God helps you,
you will be a miserable failure.*
BILL BRIGHT

A dream doesn't become a goal until it is written down.
EDWIN LOUIS COLE

*If you are bored with life—if you don't
get up every morning with a burning desire to do things—
you don't have enough goals.*
LOU HOLTZ

*You're never too old to
set a new goal or dream a new dream.*
C. S. LEWIS

More from God's Word

But if any of you lacks wisdom, let him ask of God,
who gives to all generously and without reproach,
and it will be given to him.
James 1:5 NASB

So whether you eat or drink, or whatever you do,
do it all for the glory of God.
1 Corinthians 10:31 NLT

For we are God's coworkers.
You are God's field, God's building.
1 Corinthians 3:9 HCSB

For we are His creation, created in
Christ Jesus for good works, which God prepared
ahead of time so that we should walk in them.
Ephesians 2:10 HCSB

We must do the works of Him who sent Me while it is day.
Night is coming when no one can work.
John 9:4 HCSB

A Timely Tip for Leaders

Your Goals should be SMART: Specific, Measurable, Actionable, Reachable, and Timely.

47

GOD FIRST

You shall have no other gods before Me.
EXODUS 20:3 NKJV

Wise leaders understand the importance of doing first things first. And wise Christians understand the importance of putting God first in every aspect of life, including the workplace.

If you're a Christian leader, these are very busy times. You have so many obligations and so little time. From the moment you rise until you drift off to sleep at night, you have things to do, meetings to attend, and people to contact. So how do you find time for God? You must make time for Him, plain and simple. When you put God first, you're blessed. But if you succumb to the pressures and temptations of the world, you'll inevitably pay a price.

In the book of Exodus, God warns that we should put no gods before Him. Yet all too often, we place our Lord in second, third, or fourth place as we focus on other things. When we place our desires for possessions and status above our love for God—or when we yield to the countless distractions that surround us—we forfeit the peace that might otherwise be ours.

In the wilderness, Satan offered Jesus earthly power and un-imaginable riches, but Jesus refused. Instead, He chose to worship His heavenly Father. We must do likewise by putting God first and worshiping Him only. God must come first. Always first.

Jesus Christ is the first and last, author and finisher, beginning and end, alpha and omega, and by Him all other things hold together. He must be first or nothing. God never comes next!
VANCE HAVNER

Christ is either Lord of all, or He is not Lord at all.
HUDSON TAYLOR

Worship in the truest sense takes place only when our full attention is on God—His glory, majesty, love, and compassion.
BILLY GRAHAM

To yield to God means to belong to God, and to belong to God means to have all His infinite power. To belong to God means to have all.
HANNAH WHITALL SMITH

Loving God—really loving Him—means living out His commands no matter what the cost.
CHARLES COLSON

You must never sacrifice your relationship with God for the sake of a relationship with another person.
CHARLES STANLEY

More from God's Word

*Therefore, whether you eat or drink, or whatever you do,
do all to the glory of God.*
1 Corinthians 10:31 NKJV

*For this is the love of God, that we keep His commandments.
And His commandments are not burdensome.*
1 John 5:3 NKJV

*How happy is everyone who fears the Lord,
who walks in His ways!*
Psalm 128:1 HCSB

*But prove yourselves doers of the word,
and not merely hearers who delude themselves.*
James 1:22 NASB

We love him, because he first loved us.
1 John 4:19 KJV

A Timely Tip for Leaders

As you establish priorities for your day and your life, God deserves first place. And you deserve the experience of putting Him there.

48

GOD'S CALLING

*I urge you to live a life worthy
of the calling you have received.*
EPHESIANS 4:1 NIV

God created you on purpose. He has a plan for your life that only you, as a Christian leader—with your own unique array of talents and your own particular set of circumstances—can fulfill. The Lord is gently guiding you to the place where you can accomplish the greatest good for yourself and for His kingdom.

Have you already heard God's call? And are you doing your best to pursue His plan for your life? If so, you're blessed. But if you have not yet discovered God's plan for your life, don't panic. There's still time to hear His call and follow His path. To find that path, keep searching and keep praying. Answers will come.

The Creator has placed you in a particular location, amid particular people, with particular responsibilities, and with unique opportunities to serve. And He has given you all the tools you need to accomplish His plans. So listen for His voice, watch for His signs, and prepare yourself for the call—His call—that is certain to come.

There's some task which the God of all the universe,
the great Creator, your redeemer in Jesus Christ has for you
to do, and which will remain undone and incomplete until
by faith and obedience you step into the will of God.
ALAN REDPATH

All of God's people are ordinary people who have been made
extraordinary by the purpose he has given them.
OSWALD CHAMBERS

God never calls a person into His service
without equipping him.
BILLY GRAHAM

Let God put you on His potter's wheel and
whirl you as He likes.
OSWALD CHAMBERS

Whether you have twenty years left, ten years,
one year, one month, one day, or just one hour,
there is something very important God wants you to
do that can add to His kingdom and your blessing.
BILL BRIGHT

I can't believe God put us on this earth to be ordinary.
LOU HOLTZ

MORE FROM GOD'S WORD

But as God has distributed to each one,
as the Lord has called each one, so let him walk.
1 CORINTHIANS 7:17 NKJV

And we know that all things work together
for good to those who love God, to those
who are the called according to His purpose.
ROMANS 8:28 NKJV

For whoever does the will of God is
My brother and My sister and mother.
MARK 3:35 NKJV

For many are called, but few are chosen.
MATTHEW 22:14 KJV

For you have need of endurance, so that when you have done
the will of God, you may receive what was promised.
HEBREWS 10:36 NASB

A TIMELY TIP FOR LEADERS

God has a plan for your life, a divine calling that only you can
fulfill. How you choose to respond to His calling will determine
the direction you take and the contributions you make.

49

GOD'S FORGIVENESS

*If we confess our sins, He is faithful
and righteous to forgive us our sins and to
cleanse us from all unrighteousness.*

1 JOHN 1:9 NASB

The Bible promises us that God will forgive our sins if we ask Him. It's our duty to ask; when we've fulfilled that responsibility, He will always fulfill His promise. Yet many of us continue to punish ourselves— with needless guilt and self-loathing—for mistakes that our Creator has long since forgiven and forgotten (Isaiah 43:25).

If you haven't managed to forgive yourself for some past mistake, or for a series of poor decisions, it's time to rearrange your thinking. If God has forgiven you, how can you withhold forgiveness from yourself? The answer, of course, is that God's mercy is intended to wash your sins away. That's what the Lord wants, and if you're good enough for Him, you're good enough.

*God's mercy is boundless, free, and, through Jesus Christ
our Lord, available to us in our present situation.*
A. W. TOZIER

*God does not wish us to remember
what he is willing to forget.*
GEORGE A. BUTTRICK

*Forgiveness is an opportunity that God extended to us
on the cross. When we accept His forgiveness and are
willing to forgive ourselves, then we find relief.*
BILLY GRAHAM

We cannot out-sin God's ability to forgive us.
BETH MOORE

*The most marvelous ingredient in the forgiveness of God
is that he also forgets, the one thing
a human being cannot do. With God, forgetting is
a divine attribute. God's forgiveness forgets.*
OSWALD CHAMBERS

*If God forgives us and we do not forgive ourselves,
we make ourselves greater than God.*
EDWIN LOUIS COLE

More from God's Word

*All the prophets testify about Him that through His name
everyone who believes in Him will receive forgiveness of sins.*
ACTS 10:43 HCSB

*Let us, then, feel very sure that we can come before
God's throne where there is grace. There we can receive
mercy and grace to help us when we need it.*
HEBREWS 4:16 NCV

*But the mercy of the LORD is from everlasting
to everlasting upon them that fear him,
and his righteousness unto children's children.*
PSALM 103:17 KJV

Be merciful, just as your Father is merciful.
LUKE 6:36 NIV

*It is I who sweep away your transgressions for
My own sake and remember your sins no more.*
ISAIAH 43:25 HCSB

A Timely Tip for Leaders

If you've asked for God's forgiveness, He has given it. But have
you forgiven yourself? If not, the best moment to do so is this one.

50

GOD'S GUIDANCE

*Trust in the Lord with all your heart, and lean not
on your own understanding; in all your ways
acknowledge Him, and He shall direct your paths.*

PROVERBS 3:5-6 NKJV

Leaders give guidance and receive it. And the best guidance inevitably comes from God. When we open our hearts and minds to His direction, He will lead us along a path of His choosing. But for many of us, listening to God is hard. We have so many things we want, and so many needs to pray for, that we spend far more time talking at God than we do listening to Him.

Abraham Lincoln observed, "God is the silent partner in all great enterprises." And, Oswald Chambers advised, "Get into the habit of dealing with God about everything." These words remind us that life is best lived when we seek the Lord's direction early and often.

Our Father has many ways to make Himself known. Our challenge is to make ourselves open to His instruction. So if you're unsure of your next step, trust God's promises and talk to Him often. When you do, He'll guide your steps today, tomorrow, and forever.

God is the silent partner in all great enterprises.
ABRAHAM LINCOLN

God never leads us to do anything
that is contrary to the Bible.
BILLY GRAHAM

As you walk through the valley of the unknown,
you will find the footprints of Jesus
both in front of you and beside you.
CHARLES STANLEY

When we are obedient, God guides our steps and our stops.
CORRIE TEN BOOM

The will of God will never take us
where the grace of God cannot sustain us.
BILLY GRAHAM

I am satisfied that when the Almighty wants me
to do or not to do any particular thing,
he finds a way to let me know it.
ABRAHAM LINCOLN

More from God's Word

Yet LORD, You are our Father; we are the clay,
and You are our potter; we all are the work of Your hands.
ISAIAH 64:8 HCSB

The LORD says, "I will guide you along the best pathway for
your life. I will advise you and watch over you."
PSALM 32:8 NLT

Teach me to do Your will, for You are my God;
Your Spirit is good. Lead me in the land of uprightness.
PSALM 143:10 NKJV

Shew me thy ways, O LORD; teach me thy paths.
Lead me in thy truth, and teach me: for thou art the God
of my salvation; on thee do I wait all the day.
PSALM 25:4–5 KJV

Morning by morning he wakens me and opens my
understanding to his will. The Sovereign LORD has
spoken to me, and I have listened.
ISAIAH 50:4–5 NLT

A Timely Tip for Leaders

Would you like God's guidance? Then ask Him for it. When you
pray for guidance, God will give it. So ask.

51

GOD'S PLAN

But as it is written: What eye did not see and ear did not hear,
and what never entered the human mind—
God prepared this for those who love Him.

1 CORINTHIANS 2:9 HCSB

God has a plan for this world and for your world. It's a plan that He understands perfectly, a plan that can bring you untold joy now and throughout eternity. But the Lord won't force His plan upon you. He's given you free will, the ability to make choices on your own. The totality of those choices will determine how well you fulfill God's calling.

Sometimes, God makes Himself know in obvious ways, but more often His guidance is subtle. So we must be quiet to hear His voice.

If you're serious about discovering God's plan for your life—or rediscovering it—start spending quiet time with Him every day. Ask Him for direction. Pray for clarity. And be watchful for His signs. The more time you spend with Him, the sooner the answers will come.

*You weren't an accident. You weren't mass produced.
You aren't an assembly-line product. You were
deliberately planned, specifically gifted, and lovingly
positioned on the Earth by the Master Craftsman.*

MAX LUCADO

*If not a sparrow falls upon the ground
without your Father; you have reason to see
the smallest events of your career are arranged by him.*

C. H. SPURGEON

*God's purpose is greater than our problems,
our pain and even our sin.*

RICK WARREN

*God has a course mapped out for your life, and all the
inadequacies in the world will not change His mind.
He will be with you every step of the way.*

CHARLES STANLEY

God's heavenly plan doesn't always make earthly sense.

CHARLES SWINDOLL

God has a purpose for trials and testings.

WARREN WIERSBE

More from God's Word

For My thoughts are not your thoughts, and your ways are not My ways. . . . For as heaven is higher than earth, so My ways are higher than your ways, and My thoughts than your thoughts.
ISAIAH 55:8–9 HCSB

And yet, O Lord, you are our Father. We are the clay, and you are the potter. We are all formed by your hand.
ISAIAH 64:8 NLT

For whoever does the will of God is My brother and My sister and mother.
MARK 3:35 NKJV

It is God who is at work in you, both to will and to work for His good pleasure.
PHILIPPIANS 2:13 NASB

We must do the works of Him who sent Me while it is day. Night is coming when no one can work.
JOHN 9:4 HCSB

A Timely Tip for Leaders

God has a plan for the world and for you. When you discover His plan for your life—and when you follow in the footsteps of His Son—you will be rewarded. The place where God is leading you is the place where you must go.

52

GOD'S PROMISES

Let us hold on to the confession of our hope without wavering,
for He who promised is faithful.
HEBREWS 10:23 HCSB

The Bible contains promises upon which you, as a believer, can depend. When the Creator of the universe makes a pledge to you, He will keep it. No exceptions.

You can think of the Bible as a written contract between you and your heavenly Father. When you fulfill your obligations to Him, the Lord will most certainly fulfill His covenant to you.

When we accept Christ into our hearts, God promises us the opportunity to experience contentment, peace, and spiritual abundance. But more importantly, God promises that the priceless gift of eternal life will be ours. These promises should give us comfort. With God on our side, we have absolutely nothing to fear in this world and everything to hope for in the next.

The Bible is God's book of promises,
and unlike the books of man,
it does not change or go out of date.
BILLY GRAHAM

Don't let obstacles along the road to eternity shake
your confidence in God's promises.
DAVID JEREMIAH

Faith is the assurance that the thing which
God has said in His word is true, and that God will act
according to what He has said.
GEORGE MUELLER

From one end of the Bible to the other, God assures us
that He will never go back on His promises.
BILLY GRAHAM

There are four words I wish we would never forget,
and they are, "God keeps his word."
CHARLES SWINDOLL

God is God. He knows what he is doing.
When you can't trace his hand, trust his heart.
MAX LUCADO

More from God's Word

Sustain me as You promised, and I will live;
do not let me be ashamed of my hope.
PSALM 119:116 HCSB

As for God, his way is perfect: the word of the LORD is tried:
he is a buckler to all those that trust in him.
PSALM 18:30 KJV

They will bind themselves to the LORD with an eternal
covenant that will never be forgotten.
JEREMIAH 50:5 NLT

My God is my rock, in whom I take refuge,
my shield and the horn of my salvation.
2 SAMUEL 22:2–3 NIV

He heeded their prayer, because
they put their trust in him.
1 CHRONICLES 5:20 NKJV

A Timely Tip for Leaders

God has made many promises to you, and He will keep every
single one of them. Your job is to trust God's Word and to live—
and lead—accordingly.

53

GOD'S PROTECTION

The LORD is my shepherd, I shall not want.
He makes me lie down in green pastures; He leads me
beside quiet waters. He restores my soul.
PSALM 23:1–3 NASB

God knows everything about His creation—He keeps His watchful eye on sparrows and humans alike. Whether we're in the heart of the big city, the far corner of the back forty, or anywhere in between, the Creator watches over us and protects us.

The Lord is our greatest refuge. When every earthly support system fails, He remains steadfast, and His love remains unchanged. When we encounter life's inevitable disappointments and setbacks, the Father remains faithful. When we suffer, He is always with us, always ready to respond to our prayers, always working in us and through us to turn tragedy into triumph.

Thankfully, even when there's nowhere else on earth to turn, we can turn our thoughts and prayers to the Lord, and He will respond. Even during life's most difficult days, God stands by us. Our job, of course, is to return the favor and stand by Him.

Measure the size of the obstacles against the size of God.
BETH MOORE

Only believe, don't fear. Our Master, Jesus,
always watches over us, and no matter what the persecution,
Jesus will surely overcome it.
LOTTIE MOON

A mighty fortress is our God, a bulwark never failing,
our helper he amid the flood of mortal ills prevailing.
MARTIN LUTHER

The safest place in all the world is in
the will of God, and the safest protection in all the world
is the name of God.
WARREN WIERSBE

As you walk through the valley of the unknown, you will find
the footprints of Jesus both in front of you and beside you.
CHARLES STANLEY

God is trying to get a message through to you,
and the message is: "Stop depending on inadequate
human resources. Let me handle the matter."
CATHERINE MARSHALL

MORE FROM GOD'S WORD

The LORD is my light and my salvation—
whom should I fear? The LORD is the stronghold of my life—
of whom should I be afraid?
PSALM 27:1 HCSB

As for God, His way is perfect; the word of the LORD is proven;
He is a shield to all who trust in Him.
PSALM 18:30 NKJV

The LORD is my rock, my fortress, and my deliverer, my God,
my mountain where I seek refuge. My shield, the horn of
my salvation, my stronghold, my refuge, and my Savior.
2 SAMUEL 22:2–3 HCSB

Those who trust in the LORD are like Mount Zion.
It cannot be shaken; it remains forever.
PSALM 125:1 HCSB

So we may boldly say: "The LORD is my helper;
I will not fear. What can man do to me?"
HEBREWS 13:6 NKJV

A TIMELY TIP FOR LEADERS

Earthly security is an illusion. Your only real security comes from
the loving heart of God. If you seek maximum protection, there's
only one place you can receive it: from an infinite God.

54

GOD'S TIMING

Therefore humble yourselves under the mighty hand of God,
that He may exalt you in due time.
1 PETER 5:6 NKJV

If you're like most people—and like most leaders—you're in a hurry. You know precisely what you want, and you know precisely when you want it: as soon as possible. Because your time on earth is limited, you may feel a sense of urgency. God does not. There is no panic in heaven.

Our heavenly Father, in His infinite wisdom, operates according to His own timetable, not ours. He has plans that we cannot see and purposes that we cannot know. He has created a world that unfolds according to His own schedule. Thank goodness! After all, He is omniscient; His is trustworthy; and He knows what's best for us.

If you've been waiting impatiently for the Lord to answer your prayers, it's time to put a stop to all that needless worry. You can be sure that God will answer your prayers when the time is right. You job is to keep praying—and working—until He does.

Will not the Lord's time be better than your time?
C. H. SPURGEON

*We must learn to move according to the timetable
of the Timeless One, and to be at peace.*
ELISABETH ELLIOT

*Waiting on God brings us to the journey's end
quicker than our feet.*
LETTIE COWMAN

*The Christian's journey through life
isn't a sprint but a marathon.*
BILLY GRAHAM

*Teach us, O Lord, the disciplines of patience,
for to wait is often harder than to work.*
PETER MARSHALL

*We often hear about waiting on God,
which actually means that He is waiting until we are ready.
There is another side, however. When we wait for God,
we are waiting until He is ready.*
LETTIE COWMAN

More from God's Word

He has made everything beautiful in its time.
ECCLESIASTES 3:11 NIV

He has made everything appropriate in its time. He has also put eternity in their hearts, but man cannot discover the work God has done from beginning to end.
ECCLESIASTES 3:11 HCSB

Yet the LORD longs to be gracious to you;
therefore he will rise up to show you compassion.
For the LORD is a God of justice.
Blessed are all who wait for him!
ISAIAH 30:18 NIV

Trust in the LORD with all your heart, and lean not on your own understanding; in all your ways acknowledge Him, and He shall direct your paths.
PROVERBS 3:5–6 NKJV

To every thing there is a season, and a time to every purpose under the heaven.
ECCLESIASTES 3:1 KJV

A Timely Tip for Leaders

Although you don't know precisely what you need—or when you need it—God does. So trust His timing.

55

GOD'S WILL

Teach me to do Your will, for You are my God;
Your Spirit is good. Lead me in the land of uprightness.
PSALM 143:10 NKJV

The Lord has a plan for our world and for our lives. God does not do things by accident; He has a perfect plan for His creation, a plan that includes each of us. But, because we are mortal beings with limited understanding, we can never fully comprehend the will of God. No matter. As believers in a benevolent heavenly Father, we must always trust the will of God, even though we cannot fully understand it.

As this day unfolds, seek God's will and obey His Word. When you entrust your life to Him completely and without reservation, He will give you the strength to meet any challenge, the courage to face any trial, and the wisdom to live in His righteousness and in His peace.

Life's trials are not easy. But in God's will, each has a purpose.
Often He uses them to enlarge you.
WARREN WIERSBE

To know the will of God is the highest of all wisdom.
BILLY GRAHAM

Nine-tenths of the difficulties are overcome
when our hearts are ready to do the Lord's will.
GEORGE MUELLER

God has a present will for your life. It is neither
chaotic nor utterly exhausting. In the midst of
many good choices vying for your time, He will give you
the discernment to recognize what is best.
BETH MOORE

I do not need to feel good or be ecstatic
in order to be in the center of God's will.
BILL BRIGHT

It is possible to see God's will in every circumstance and to
accept it with singing instead of complaining.
LETTIE COWMAN

More from God's Word

Commit to the Lord whatever you do,
and your plans will succeed.
PROVERBS 16:3 NIV

For it is God who is working in you, enabling you both
to desire and to work out His good purpose.
PHILIPPIANS 2:13 HCSB

Then Jesus explained: "My nourishment comes from doing the
will of God, who sent me, and from finishing his work."
JOHN 4:34 NLT

For it is better, if it is the will of God,
to suffer for doing good than for doing evil.
1 PETER 3:17 NKJV

He is the Lord. He will do what He thinks is good.
1 SAMUEL 3:18 HCSB

A Timely Tip for Leaders

Even when you cannot understand God's plans, you must trust them. If you place yourself in the center of God's will, He will provide for your needs and direct your path.

56

HELPING OTHERS

*Carry one another's burdens; in this way
you will fulfill the law of Christ.*
GALATIANS 6:2 HCSB

Servant-leaders are in the business of helping others. And, if you're looking for somebody to help, you won't have to look very far. Somebody very nearby needs a helping hand or a hot meal or a pat on the back or a prayer. In order to find that person, you'll need to keep your eyes and your heart open, and you'll need to stay focused on the needs of others. Focusing, however, is not as simple as it seems.

We live in a fast-paced, media-driven world filled with countless temptations and time-wasting distractions. Sometimes, we may convince ourselves that we simply don't have the time or the resources to offer help to the needy. Such thoughts are misguided. Caring for our neighbors must be *our* priority because it is *God's* priority.

God has placed you here and given you particular responsibilities. He has a specific plan for your life, and part of that plan involves service to coworkers, teammates, friends, family members, and complete strangers. Service, like leadership, is not a burden; it's an opportunity. Seize your opportunity today. Tomorrow may be too late.

A true servant of God is one who helps another succeed.
BILLY GRAHAM

*What does love look like? It has the hands to help others.
It has the feet to hasten to the poor and needy. It has
eyes to see misery and want. It has the ears to hear the sighs
and sorrows of men. That is what love looks like.*
ST. AUGUSTINE

*The measure of a life, after all,
is not its duration but its donation.*
CORRIE TEN BOOM

Don't waste your pain; use it to help others.
RICK WARREN

*Do all the good you can, by all the means you can,
in all the places you can, at all the times you can,
to all the people you can, as long as ever you can.*
JOHN WESLEY

He climbs highest who helps another up.
ZIG ZIGLAR

MORE FROM GOD'S WORD

*Let us not become weary in doing good, for at the proper time
we will reap a harvest if we do not give up.*
GALATIANS 6:9 NIV

Whenever you are able, do good to people who need help.
PROVERBS 3:27 NCV

*If you have two shirts, give one to the poor. If you have food,
share it with those who are hungry.*
LUKE 3:11 NLT

*Whatever you did for one of the least of
these brothers of Mine, you did for Me.*
MATTHEW 25:40 HCSB

*Therefore, as we have opportunity, we must
work for the good of all, especially for those who
belong to the household of faith.*
GALATIANS 6:10 HCSB

A TIMELY TIP FOR LEADERS

*Life's most persistent and urgent question is,
"What are we doing for others?"*
MARTIN LUTHER KING JR.

57

HOPE

Let us hold fast the confession of our hope without wavering,
for He who promised is faithful.

HEBREWS 10:23 NASB

God's promises give us hope: hope for today, hope for tomorrow, hope for all eternity. The hope that the world offers is temporary, at best. But the hope that God offers never grows old and never goes out of date. It's no wonder, then, that when we pin our hopes on worldly resources, we are often disappointed. Thankfully, God has no such record of failure.

The Bible teaches that the Lord blesses those who trust in His wisdom and follow in the footsteps of His Son. Will you count yourself among that number? When you do, you'll have every reason on earth—and in heaven—to be hopeful about your future. After all, God has made important promises to you, promises that He is certainly going to keep. So be hopeful, be optimistic, be faithful, and do your best. Then, leave the rest up to God. Your destiny is safe with Him.

Jesus gives us hope because He keeps us company,
has a vision and knows the way we should go.
MAX LUCADO

The presence of hope in the invincible
sovereignty of God drives out fear.
JOHN PIPER

The earth's troubles fade in the light of heaven's hope.
BILLY GRAHAM

If your hopes are being disappointed just now,
it means that they are being purified.
OSWALD CHAMBERS

Never yield to gloomy anticipation.
Place your hope and confidence in God.
He has no record of failure.
LETTIE COWMAN

Great hopes make great men.
THOMAS FULLER

More from God's Word

This hope we have as an anchor of the soul,
a hope both sure and steadfast.
HEBREWS 6:19 NASB

I say to myself, "The LORD is mine, so I hope in him."
LAMENTATIONS 3:24 NCV

The LORD is good to those who wait for Him,
to the soul who seeks Him. It is good that one should hope
and wait quietly for the salvation of the LORD.
LAMENTATIONS 3:25–26 NKJV

Hope deferred makes the heart sick.
PROVERBS 13:12 NKJV

Be strong and courageous,
all you who put your hope in the LORD.
PSALM 31:24 HCSB

A Timely Tip for Leaders

If you're experiencing tough times, remember that other leaders have faced similar situations. They made it, and so can you. If you do your part, God will do his part. So never be afraid to hope—or to ask—for a miracle.

58

HUMILITY

Therefore humble yourselves under the mighty hand of God,
that He may exalt you in due time, casting
all your care upon Him, for He cares for you.
1 PETER 5:6–7 NKJV

We humans are often tempted by a dangerous, debilitating sin: pride. Even though God's Word clearly warns us that pride is hazardous to our spiritual health, we're still tempted to brag about our accomplishments, and overstate them. We're tempted to puff ourselves up by embellishing our victories and concealing our defeats. But in truth, all of us are mere mortals who have many more reasons to be humble than prideful.

As Christians who have been saved, not by our own good works but by God's grace, how can we be prideful? The answer, of course, is that if we are honest with ourselves and with our God we simply can't be boastful. We must, instead, be filled with humble appreciation for the things God has done. Our good works are miniscule compared to His. Whatever happens, the Lord deserves the credit, not us. And, if we're wise, we'll give Him all the credit He deserves.

Humility is not thinking less of yourself,
it's thinking of yourself less.
RICK WARREN

God measures people by the small dimensions of
humility and not by the bigness of their achievements
or the size of their capabilities.
BILLY GRAHAM

The holy man is the most humble man you can meet.
OSWALD CHAMBERS

Not until we have become humble and teachable,
standing in awe of God's holiness and sovereignty,
distrusting our own thoughts, and willing to have our minds
turned upside down, can divine wisdom become ours.
J. I. PACKER

A man wrapped up in himself
makes a very small package.
BEN FRANKLIN

Faith itself cannot be strong where humility is weak.
C. H. SPURGEON

More from God's Word

Always be humble, gentle, and patient,
accepting each other in love.
Ephesians 4:2 NCV

Humble yourselves in the sight of the Lord,
and he shall lift you up.
James 4:10 KJV

For everyone who exalts himself will be humbled,
and the one who humbles himself will be exalted.
Luke 14:11 HCSB

Therefore, God's chosen ones, holy and loved,
put on heartfelt compassion, kindness,
humility, gentleness, and patience.
Colossians 3:12 HCSB

Blessed are the meek: for they shall inherit the earth.
Matthew 5:5 KJV

A Timely Tip for Leaders

God favors the humble just as surely as He disciplines the proud. Humility leads to contentment; pride doesn't. Act—and lead—accordingly.

59

JOY

This is the day which the LORD has made;
let us rejoice and be glad in it.
PSALM 118:24 NASB

The joy that the world offers is fleeting and incomplete: here today, gone tomorrow, not coming back anytime soon. But God's joy is different. His joy has staying power. In fact, it's a gift that never stops giving to those who welcome His Son into their hearts.

Psalm 100 reminds us to celebrate the lives that God has given us: "Shout for joy to the LORD, all the earth. Worship the LORD with gladness; come before him with joyful songs." (vv. 1–2 NIV). Yet sometimes, amid the inevitable complications and predicaments that are woven into the fabric of everyday life, we forget to rejoice. Instead of celebrating life, we complain about it. This is an understandable mistake, but a mistake nonetheless. As Christians, we are called by our Creator to live joyfully and abundantly. To do otherwise is to squander His spiritual gifts.

This day and every day, Christ offers you His peace and His joy. Accept it and share it with others, just as He has shared His joy with you.

No one can get Joy by merely asking for it.
It is one of the ripest fruits of the Christian life, and,
like all fruits, must be grown.
HENRY DRUMMOND

Joy is the direct result of having God's perspective on our
daily lives and the effect of loving our Lord enough to
obey His commands and trust His promises.
BILL BRIGHT

Joy comes not from what we have but what we are.
C. H. SPURGEON

Joy is the great note all throughout the Bible.
OSWALD CHAMBERS

Joy is the settled assurance that God is in control of all
the details of my life, the quiet confidence that ultimately
everything is going to be all right, and the determined choice to
praise God in all things.
KAY WARREN

Joy is the serious business of heaven.
C. S. LEWIS

MORE FROM GOD'S WORD

Rejoice in the Lord always. Again I will say, rejoice!
PHILIPPIANS 4:4 NKJV

Rejoice always, pray without ceasing, in everything give thanks;
for this is the will of God in Christ Jesus for you.
1 THESSALONIANS 5:16–18 NKJV

I have spoken these things to you so that My joy
may be in you and your joy may be complete.
JOHN 15:11 HCSB

Until now you have asked for nothing in My name.
Ask and you will receive, that your joy may be complete.
JOHN 16:24 HCSB

So you also have sorrow now. But I will see you again.
Your hearts will rejoice, and no one will rob you of your joy.
JOHN 16:22 HCSB

A TIMELY TIP FOR LEADERS

Joy does not depend upon your circumstances; it depends upon your thoughts and upon your relationship with God. Every day, God gives you many reasons to rejoice. The gifts are His, but the rejoicing is up to you.

60

KINDNESS AND COMPASSION

Therefore, whatever you want men to do to you, do also to them, for this is the Law and the Prophets.

MATTHEW 7:12 NKJV

Jesus set the example: He was compassionate, loving, and kind. If we, as Christian leaders, seek to follow Him, we, too, must combine compassionate hearts with willing hands.

John Wesley's said: "Do all the good you can, by all the means you can, in all the places you can, at all the times you can, to all the people you can, as long as ever you can." His advice still applies. In order to follow in Christ's footsteps, we must be compassionate. There is simply no other way.

Never underestimate the power of kindness. You never know when a kind word or gesture might significantly improve someone's day, or week, or life. So be quick to offer words of encouragement, and smiles, and pats on the back. Be generous with your resources and your time. Make kindness the cornerstone of your dealings with others. They will be blessed, and you will be, too. And everybody wins.

All around you are people whose lives are filled with trouble and sorrow. They need your compassion and encouragement.
BILLY GRAHAM

Want to snatch a day from the manacles of boredom? Do overgenerous deeds, acts beyond reimbursement. Kindness without compensation. Do a deed for which you cannot be repaid.
MAX LUCADO

One of the greatest things a man can do for his Heavenly Father is to be kind to some of His other children.
HENRY DRUMMOND

When we bring sunshine into the lives of others, we're warmed by it ourselves. When we spill a little happiness, it splashes on us.
BARBARA JOHNSON

If my heart is right with God, every human being is my neighbor.
OSWALD CHAMBERS

Kind words are the music of the world.
FREDERICK W. FABER

More from God's Word

A new commandment I give unto you, That ye love one another;
as I have loved you, that ye also love one another.
JOHN 13:34 KJV

Who is wise and understanding among you?
He should show his works by good conduct
with wisdom's gentleness.
JAMES 3:13 HCSB

Be kind to one another, tender-hearted, forgiving each other,
just as God in Christ also has forgiven you.
EPHESIANS 4:32 NASB

And let us not grow weary while doing good, for in due season
we shall reap if we do not lose heart.
GALATIANS 6:9 NKJV

Assuredly, I say to you, inasmuch as you did it to one of
the least of these My brethren, you did it to Me.
MATTHEW 25:40 NKJV

A Timely Tip for Leaders

Kindness is contagious. So make sure that your family, friends, coworkers, and even strangers, catch it from you!

61

KNOWLEDGE

Wisdom is the principal thing; therefore get wisdom.
And in all your getting, get understanding.
PROVERBS 4:7 NKJV

What does it take to become wise? Experience helps. So does education. Common sense helps, and mentors help, too. But the best wisdom, and the most important, is found between the covers of the book God wrote. So, if you sincerely desire to become wise, you must begin by studying His Word. In it, you'll find everything you need to live wisely and well.

Warren Wiersbe observed that, "Wise people listen to wise instruction, especially instruction from the Word of God." Savvy Christian leaders agree.

So, if you need technical knowledge, grab a textbook or take a class. And, if you need more education, go back to school. But, if you're searching for eternal truths—the kind of wisdom that doesn't change with the shifting tides of popular opinion—the best way to start is by opening your Bible and opening your heart to God. When you do, you'll discover that His wisdom always applies and His guidance never fails.

The wisest mind has something yet to learn.
GEORGE SANTAYANA

Life is not a holiday but an education. And, the one eternal lesson for all of us is how we can love.
HENRY DRUMMOND

Being ignorant is not so much a shame as being unwilling to learn.
BEN FRANKLIN

A time of trouble and darkness is meant to teach you lessons you desperately need.
LETTIE COWMAN

Wisdom is the right use of knowledge. To know is not to be wise. There is no fool so great as the knowing fool. But, to know how to use knowledge is to have wisdom.
C. H. SPURGEON

I am still learning, for the Christian life is one of constant growth.
BILLY GRAHAM

More from God's Word

Commit yourself to instruction;
listen carefully to words of knowledge.
PROVERBS 23:12 NLT

Enthusiasm without knowledge is not good.
If you act too quickly, you might make a mistake.
PROVERBS 19:2 NCV

Joyful is the person who finds wisdom,
the one who gains understanding.
PROVERBS 3:13 NLT

Teach me Your way, Yahweh, and I will live by Your truth.
Give me an undivided mind to fear Your name.
PSALM 86:11 HCSB

Anyone who listens to my teaching and follows it is wise, like a
person who builds a house on solid rock. Though the rain comes
in torrents and the floodwaters rise and the winds beat against
that house, it won't collapse, because it is built on built on bedrock.
MATTHEW 7:24 NLT

A Timely Tip for Leaders

The only people who achieve much are those who want
knowledge so badly that they seek it while the conditions
are still unfavorable. Favorable conditions never come.
C. S. LEWIS

62

LEADERSHIP

A good leader plans to do good,
and those good things make him a good leader.
ISAIAH 32:8 NCV

The world defines leadership in many ways, oftentimes using vague platitudes and general descriptions. But God's definition is more specific. He's looking for servant-leaders who are willing to follow in the footsteps of His only begotten Son. And, He's always willing to help those men and women who genuinely place His priorities first.

If you're seriously considering Christian leadership, then you must be equally serious about Christian service. After all, Jesus Himself came, not as a conquering autocrat but as a humble servant. For those who seek to follow Him—and lead others along that same path—a genuine commitment to service is not optional. It's required.

*A leader is one who knows the way, goes the way,
and shows the way.*
JOHN MAXWELL

*Leaders become great, not because of their power,
but because of their ability to empower others.*
JOHN MAXWELL

Servanthood does not nullify leadership; it defines it.
JOHN PIPER

*According to Scripture, virtually everything that
truly qualifies a person for leadership is directly related
to character. Integrity is the main issue that makes
the difference between a good leader and a bad one.*
JOHN MACARTHUR

*A great leader's courage to fulfill his vision
comes from passion, not position.*
JOHN MAXWELL

*A true shepherd leads the way.
He does not merely point the way.*
LEONARD RAVENHILL

MORE FROM GOD'S WORD

Shepherd the flock of God which is among you.
1 PETER 5:2 NKJV

An overseer, therefore, must be above reproach,
the husband of one wife, self-controlled, sensible,
respectable, hospitable, an able teacher, not addicted to wine,
not a bully but gentle, not quarrelsome, not greedy.
1 TIMOTHY 3:2–3 HCSB

Those who are wise will shine like the
brightness of the heavens, and those who lead many
to righteousness, like the stars for ever and ever.
DANIEL 12:3 NIV

Therefore encourage one another and build up one another,
just as you also are doing.
1 THESSALONIANS 5:11 NASB

Good leaders cultivate honest speech;
they love advisors who tell them the truth.
PROVERBS 16:13 MSG

A TIMELY TIP FOR LEADERS

If you want to be a godly leader, you must first learn to be a faithful follower—a follower of the man from Galilee. Once you've learned to walk with Jesus, you'll be ready to lead others by your words and, more importantly, by your example.

63

LIFE

*I urge you to live a life worthy of
the calling you have received.*
EPHESIANS 4:1 NIV

Life is God's gift to you, and He intends for you to celebrate His glorious gift. So if you're a Christian leader who treasures each day—and if you're enthusiastically encouraging others to do likewise—congratulations, you're doing God's will.

For thoughtful Christians, every day begins and ends with God and His Son. Believers who fashion their days around Jesus are transformed: They see the world differently; they behave differently; and, they feel differently about themselves and their neighbors. Faithful believers face the inevitable challenges of everyday life armed with the joy of Christ and the promise of salvation. So whatever this day holds for you, begin it and end it with God as your partner and Christ as your Savior. And throughout the day, give thanks to your Creator. God's love for you is infinite. Accept it joyfully and be thankful.

Jesus wants Life for us;
Life with a capital L.
JOHN ELDREDGE

Live out your life in its full meaning; it is God's life.
JOSIAH ROYCE

Wherever you are, be all there. Live to the hilt
every situation you believe to be the will of God.
JIM ELLIOT

The measure of a life, after all,
is not its duration but its donation.
CORRIE TEN BOOM

You have life before you.
Only you can live it.
HENRY DRUMMOND

You can't control the length of your life—
but you can control its width and depth.
JOHN MAXWELL

More from God's Word

Jesus said to her, "I am the resurrection and the life.
The one who believes in Me, even if he dies, will live.
Everyone who lives and believes in Me will never die—
ever. Do you believe this?"
John 11:25–26 HCSB

And Jesus said unto them, I am the bread of life:
he that cometh to me shall never hunger;
and he that believeth on me shall never thirst.
John 6:35 KJV

He who follows righteousness and mercy
finds life, righteousness and honor.
Proverbs 21:21 NKJV

Whoever finds their life will lose it, and whoever
loses their life for my sake will find it.
Matthew 10:39 NIV

You will teach me how to live a holy life. Being with you will
fill me with joy; at your right hand I will find pleasure forever.
Psalm 16:11 NCV

A Timely Tip for Leaders

Your life is a priceless opportunity, a gift of incalculable worth. Be thankful to the Giver and use His gift wisely while there's still time because night is coming when no one can work.

64

LISTENING TO GOD

Be still, and know that I am God.
PSALM 46:10 KJV

God speaks to us in different ways at different times. Sometimes He speaks loudly and clearly. But more often, He speaks in a quiet voice—and if you seek to be a wise leader, you will be listening carefully when He does. To do so, you must carve out quiet moments each day to study His Word and to sense His direction.

Are you willing to pray sincerely and then to wait quietly for God's response? Can you quiet yourself long enough to listen to your conscience? Are you attuned to the subtle guidance of your intuition? Hopefully so. Usually God refrains from sending His messages on stone tablets or city billboards. More often, He communicates in subtler ways. If you sincerely desire to hear His voice, you must listen carefully, and you must do so in the silent corners of your quiet, willing heart.

When God speaks to us, He should have our full attention.
BILLY GRAHAM

Prayer begins by talking to God, but it ends in listening to him.
In the face of Absolute Truth, silence is the soul's language.
FULTON J. SHEEN

God's voice is still and quiet and
easily buried under an avalanche of clamor.
CHARLES STANLEY

Some of us can only hear God in the thunder of revivals
or in public worship; we have to learn to listen
to God's voice in the ordinary circumstances of life.
OSWALD CHAMBERS

Prayer is speaking to God, but sometimes He uses our times
of prayerful silence to speak to us in return.
BILLY GRAHAM

God speaks through a variety of means. In the present God
primarily speaks by the Holy Spirit, through the Bible, prayer,
circumstances, and the church.
HENRY BLACKABY

More from God's Word

In quietness and in confidence shall be your strength.
ISAIAH 30:15 KJV

Rest in the LORD, and wait patiently for Him.
PSALM 37:7 NKJV

Listen, listen to me, and eat what is good, and you will delight in the richest of fare. Give ear and come to me; listen, that you may live.
ISAIAH 55:2-3 NIV

The one who is from God listens to God's words. This is why you don't listen, because you are not from God.
JOHN 8:47 HCSB

Be silent before Me.
ISAIAH 41:1 HCSB

A Timely Tip for Leaders

If you want to have a meaningful conversation with God, don't make Him shout. Instead, go to a quiet place and listen. If you keep listening long enough and carefully enough, the Lord will talk directly to you.

65

MENTORS

A wise man will hear and increase learning,
and a man of understanding will attain wise counsel.
PROVERBS 1:5 NKJV

The Roman playwright Plautus said, "None of us are wise enough by ourselves." What was true in 200 BC is still true today. In today's fast-changing world, we need the benefit of good counsel, informed opinions, and honest advice.

Even the wisest leaders can't be successful by themselves. They need trustworthy mentors and competent counselors. And, if you wish to become a skilled leader, you'll need advisors, too.

So, the next time you're facing a big decision, don't be too proud to ask for advice. Then, when you've sought the opinions of people you trust, consult the ultimate Counselor: your Father in heaven. With His guidance, and with the help of trusted friends and mentors, you can make important decisions with confidence.

You're never too young to be taught
and never too old to teach.
EDWIN LOUIS COLE

A friend is one who makes me do my best.
OSWALD CHAMBERS

God send me a friend that will tell me of my faults.
THOMAS FULLER

Few delights can equal the presence
of one whom we trust utterly.
GEORGE MACDONALD

True wisdom is marked by willingness to listen
and a sense of knowing when to yield.
ELIZABETH GEORGE

Be with wise men and become wiser.
Be with foolish men and become foolish.
EDWIN LOUIS COLE

More from God's Word

Listen to advice and accept correction,
and in the end you will be wise.
PROVERBS 19:20 NCV

How much better to get wisdom than gold,
to get insight rather than silver!
PROVERBS 16:16 NIV

Those who are wise shall shine like the
brightness of the firmament, and those who turn many
to righteousness like the stars forever and ever.
DANIEL 12:3 NKJV

Iron sharpens iron, and one man sharpens another.
PROVERBS 27:17 HCSB

A fool's way is right in his own eyes,
but whoever listens to counsel is wise.
PROVERBS 12:15 HCSB

A Timely Tip for Leaders

When it comes to mentors, you need them. When it comes to mentoring, they need you.

66

MIRACLES

Is anything too hard for the LORD?
GENESIS 18:14 NKJV

God's power has no limitations. He is not restrained by the laws of nature because He created those laws. At any time, at any place, under any set of circumstances, He can accomplish anything He chooses. The things that seem miraculous to us are, to Him, expressions of His power and His love.

Do you expect God to work miracles in your own life? You should. From the moment He created our universe out of nothingness, the Lord has made a habit of doing miraculous things. And He's still working miracles today.

With God nothing is impossible. His wondrous works come in all shapes and sizes, so keep your eyes and your heart open. Somewhere, a miracle is about to happen, and it might just happen *to you*.

The same Jesus Who turned water into wine can
transform your home, your life, your family, and your future.
He is still in the miracle-working business,
and His business is the business of transformation.
ADRIAN ROGERS

God is able to do what we can't do.
BILLY GRAHAM

Consider Jesus. Know Jesus. Learn what kind of Person it is you
say you trust and love and worship. Soak in the shadow
of Jesus. Saturate your soul with the ways of Jesus. Watch Him.
Listen to Him. Stand in awe of Him.
JOHN PIPER

Are you looking for a miracle? If you keep your eyes wide open
and trust in God, you won't have to look very far.
MARIE T. FREEMAN

God's specialty is raising dead things to life
and making impossible things possible.
You don't have the need that exceeds His power.
BETH MOORE

We honor God by asking for great things when they are a part
of His promise. We dishonor Him and cheat ourselves when we
ask for molehills where He has promised mountains.
VANCE HAVNER

More from God's Word

*And God confirmed the message by
giving signs and wonders and various miracles
and gifts of the Holy Spirit whenever he chose.*
HEBREWS 2:4 NLT

*What no eye has seen, what no ear has heard,
and what no human mind has conceived"—
the things God has prepared for those who love him.*
1 CORINTHIANS 2:9 NIV

*You are the God of great wonders!
You demonstrate your awesome power among the nations.*
PSALM 77:14 NLT

*And Jesus looking upon them saith, With men it is impossible,
but not with God: for with God all things are possible.*
MARK 10:27 KJV

For with God nothing shall be impossible.
LUKE 1:37 KJV

A Timely Tip for Leaders

God has infinite power. Nothing is impossible for Him. If you're watchful, you'll observe many miracles. So keep your eyes, your heart, and your mind open.

67

MISTAKES

If we confess our sins to him, he is faithful and just
to forgive us and to cleanse us from every wrong.
1 JOHN 1:9 NLT

None of us are perfect; we all make mistakes. The question, then, is not *whether* we'll make mistakes, but *what* we'll do about them. If we focus on covering up instead of fixing, we invite even more troubles. But if we learn from our mistakes and make amends whenever possible, God will help us make use of our setbacks.

Have you recently made a mistake that caused trouble, disappointment, or heartbreak? If so, look for the lesson that the Lord is trying to teach you. Instead of grumbling about life's sad state of affairs, learn what needs to be learned, change what needs to be changed, and move on. View every major setback as an opportunity to reassess God's will for your life. And while you're at it, consider your mistakes to be powerful opportunities to learn more about yourself, your circumstances, and your world.

Everybody (including you) makes mistakes. Your job is to make them only once. And with God's help, you can do it.

A man must be big enough
to admit his mistakes, smart enough to profit from them,
and strong enough to correct them.
JOHN MAXWELL

Show me a man who doesn't make mistakes
and I'll show you a man who doesn't do anything.
THEODORE ROOSEVELT

In your relationship with God, He may let you make a wrong
decision. Then the Spirit of God causes you to recognize that it
is not God's will. He guides you back to the right path.
HENRY BLACKABY

A stumble may prevent a fall.
THOMAS FULLER

Goals are worth setting and worth missing.
We learn from non-successes.
BILL BRIGHT

If you're not making mistakes, then you're not doing anything.
I'm positive that a doer makes mistakes.
JOHN WOODEN

More from God's Word

*He who covers his sins will not prosper, but whoever
confesses and forsakes them will have mercy.*
PROVERBS 28:13 NKJV

*Therefore let us approach the throne of grace with boldness,
so that we may receive mercy and find grace
to help us at the proper time.*
HEBREWS 4:16 HCSB

*But the mercy of the LORD is from everlasting to everlasting
upon them that fear him, and his righteousness
unto children's children.*
PSALM 103:17 KJV

Be merciful, just as your Father is merciful.
LUKE 6:36 NIV

*Therefore, if anyone is in Christ, he is a new creation;
old things have passed away;
behold, all things have become new.*
2 CORINTHIANS 5:17 NKJV

A Timely Tip for Leaders

Everybody makes mistakes, and so will you. And when it comes to
repairing those mistakes, sooner beats later. So ask yourself, "If not
now, when?"

68

MOTIVATING OTHERS

The hearts of the wise make their mouths prudent,
and their lips promote instruction.
PROVERBS 16:23 NIV

The best leaders find ways to motivate the people around them. How do they do it? With integrity, with clarity, with encouragement and hope.

Each day provides countless opportunities to encourage family, friends, and coworkers by praising their good works and acknowledging their accomplishments. When we do, we spread seeds of optimism and hope in a world that needs both.

In his letter to the Ephesians, Paul writes, "Do not let any unwholesome talk come out of your mouths, but only what is helpful for building others up according to their needs, that it may benefit those who listen" (4:29 NIV). These words remind us that when we choose our words carefully and well, we honor the One who gave His life for us.

Leaders become great, not because of their power,
but because of their ability to empower others.
JOHN MAXWELL

The strength of the group is the strength of the leader.
VINCE LOMBARDI

I am an optimist. It does not seem
to be much use being anything else.
WINSTON CHURCHILL

Praise loudly. Criticize softly.
LOU HOLTZ

A spoonful of honey will catch more flies
than a gallon of vinegar.
BEN FRANKLIN

Leadership is the knack of getting somebody to do something
you want done because he wants to do it.
DWIGHT D. EISENHOWER

More from God's Word

*A word spoken at the right time is like
golden apples on a silver tray.*
PROVERBS 25:11 HCSB

*Now finally, all of you should be like-minded and sympathetic,
should love believers, and be compassionate and humble.*
1 PETER 3:8 HCSB

*But encourage one another day after day, as long as it is still
called "Today," so that none of you will be hardened by the
deceitfulness of sin.*
HEBREWS 3:13 NASB

*Therefore encourage one another and
build each other up as you are already doing.*
1 THESSALONIANS 5:11 HCSB

*Let the words of my mouth and the
meditation of my heart be acceptable in Your sight,
O LORD, my strength and my Redeemer.*
PSALM 19:14 NKJV

A Timely Tip for Leaders

*You can motivate by fear. And you can motivate by reward.
But those methods are temporary.
The only lasting motivation is self-motivation.*
HOMER SMITH

69

OBEDIENCE

Now by this we know that we know Him,
if we keep His commandments.
1 JOHN 2:3 NKJV

Leaders expect obedience from their followers. And God expects no less from us. His instructions, which are contained in the Holy Bible, are given for our own benefit. When we obey God's commandments and listen carefully to the conscience He has placed in our hearts, we are secure. But if we disobey our Creator, if we choose to ignore the teachings and the warnings of His Word, we do so at great peril.

Billy Graham offered this warning: "The Bible teaches that when we turn our backs on God and choose to disregard His moral laws there are inevitable consequences." These words serve as a powerful reminder that, as Christians, we are called to take God's promises seriously and to live in accordance with His teachings.

God gave us His commandments for a reason: so that we might obey them and be blessed. Yet we live in a world that presents us with countless temptations to stray far from His path. It is our responsibility to resist those temptations with vigor. Obedience isn't just the best way to experience the full measure of God's blessings; it's the only way.

One act of obedience is better than one hundred sermons.
DIETRICH BONHOEFFER

*The golden rule for understanding in spiritual matters
is not intellect, but obedience.*
OSWALD CHAMBERS

*Faith and obedience are bound up in the same bundle.
He that obeys God, trusts God;
and he that trusts God, obeys God.*
C. H. SPURGEON

*God has laid down spiritual laws which,
if obeyed, bring harmony and fulfillment,
but, if disobeyed, bring discord and disorder.*
BILLY GRAHAM

When we are obedient, God guides our steps and our stops.
CORRIE TEN BOOM

*It is only by obedience that we
understand the teaching of God.*
OSWALD CHAMBERS

More from God's Word

We must obey God rather than men.
ACTS 5:29 NASB

Teach me, O LORD, the way of Your statutes,
and I shall observe it to the end.
PSALM 119:33 NASB

Trust in the LORD with all your heart, and lean not
on your own understanding; in all your ways
acknowledge Him, and He shall direct your paths.
PROVERBS 3:5–6 NKJV

Praise the LORD! Happy are those who respect the LORD,
who want what he commands.
PSALM 112:1 NCV

But prove yourselves doers of the word,
and not merely hearers who delude themselves.
JAMES 1:22 NASB

A Timely Tip for Leaders

Because God is just, He rewards good behavior just as surely as
He punishes sin. Obedience earns God's pleasure; disobedience
doesn't. Behave—and lead—accordingly.

70

OPPORTUNITIES

Remember ye not the former things, neither consider the things of old. Behold, I will do a new thing.
ISAIAH 43:18–19 KJV

Savvy leaders are constantly searching for opportunities, and not surprisingly, they often find what they're looking for.

As you consider the trajectory of your career—and as you consider your opportunities for leadership—do you see possibilities, opportunities, and blessings from above? Or do you focus on stumbling blocks instead of stepping stones?

If you're consistently looking for opportunities, you'll discover that opportunities have a way of turning up in the most unexpected places. But, if you've acquired the unfortunate habit of looking for problems instead of possibilities, you'll find that troubles have a way of turning up in unexpected places, too.

Since you're likely to find what you're looking for, why not look for opportunities? They're out there. And the rest is up to you.

When God closes one door,
He often opens another—if we seek it.
BILLY GRAHAM

We are all faced with a series of great opportunities
brilliantly disguised as impossible situations.
CHARLES SWINDOLL

The past is our teacher; the present is our opportunity;
the future is our friend.
EDWIN LOUIS COLE

A possibility is a hint from God.
SØREN KIERKEGAARD

Opportunity is missed by most people because it is
dressed in overalls and looks like work.
HENRY J. KAISER, JR.

Difficulties mastered are opportunities won.
WINSTON CHURCHILL

MORE FROM GOD'S WORD

But as it is written:
What eye did not see and ear did not hear,
and what never entered the human mind—
God prepared this for those who love Him.
1 CORINTHIANS 2:9 HCSB

Whenever we have the opportunity, we should do good to
everyone—especially to those in the family of faith
GALATIANS 6:10 NLT

I can do all things through Christ which strengtheneth me.
PHILIPPIANS 4:13 KJV

I remind you to fan into flame the gift of God.
2 TIMOTHY 1:6 NIV

But those who wait on the LORD shall renew their strength;
they shall mount up with wings like eagles, they shall run
and not be weary, they shall walk and not faint.
ISAIAH 40:31 NKJV

A TIMELY TIP FOR LEADERS

Every opportunity has an expiration date. Your challenge is to discover the opportunities that God has placed before you—and to make the most of those opportunities—before they expire.

71

OPTIMISM

The LORD is my light and my salvation—
whom should I fear? The LORD is the stronghold of my life—
of whom should I be afraid?
PSALM 27:1 HCSB

Are you a passionate Christian who expects God to do big things in your life and in the lives of those around you? If you're a thinking Christian, you have every reason to be confident about your future here on earth and your eternal future in heaven. As English clergyman William Ralph Inge observed, "No Christian should be a pessimist, for Christianity is a system of radical optimism." Inge's observation is true, of course, but sometimes, you may find yourself caught up in the inevitable complications of everyday living. When you find yourself fretting about the inevitable ups and downs of life here on earth, it's time to slow down, collect yourself, refocus your thoughts, and count your blessings.

God has made promises to you, and He will most certainly keep every one of them. So, you have every reason to be an optimist and no legitimate reason to ever abandon hope.

Today, trust your hopes, not your fears. And while you're at it, take time to celebrate God's blessings. His gifts are too numerous to calculate and too glorious to imagine. But, it never hurts to try.

Two types of voices command your attention today.
Negative ones fill your mind with doubt, bitterness, and fear.
Positive ones purvey hope and strength.
Which one will you choose to heed?

MAX LUCADO

When you have vision it affects your attitude.
Your attitude is optimistic rather than pessimistic.

CHARLES SWINDOLL

Positive thinking will let you do everything
better than negative thinking will.

ZIG ZIGLAR

I am an optimist. It does not seem
to be much use being anything else.

WINSTON CHURCHILL

Things turn out best for the people
who make the best of the way things turn out.

JOHN WOODEN

Never yield to gloomy anticipation. Place your hope and
confidence in God. He has no record of failure.

LETTIE COWMAN

More from God's Word

Make me to hear joy and gladness.
PSALM 51:8 KJV

But if we look forward to something we don't have yet,
we must wait patiently and confidently.
ROMANS 8:25 NLT

"I say this because I know what I am planning for you,"
says the LORD. "I have good plans for you, not plans to hurt
you.
I will give you hope and a good future."
JEREMIAH 29:11 NCV

This hope we have as an anchor of the soul,
a hope both sure and steadfast.
HEBREWS 6:19 NASB

Let us hold on to the confession of our hope without wavering,
for He who promised is faithful.
HEBREWS 10:23 HCSB

A Timely Tip for Leaders

As a Christian leader, you have every reason to be optimistic about your future here on earth and your future in heaven. God is good, and your eternal future is secure. So why not be an optimist?

72

PAST

Do not remember the former things, nor consider the things of old. Behold, I will do a new thing.
ISAIAH 43:18–19 NKJV

As a Christian leader, you should learn from the past, but you shouldn't live there. Sometimes, that's easier said than done. Yesterday's blunders are hard to forget, and past disappointments will sidetrack us if we let them.

Since we can't change the pains and disappointments of the past, why do so many of us insist upon replaying them over and over again in our minds? Perhaps it's because we can't find it in our hearts to forgive the people who have hurt us. Being mere mortals, we seek revenge, not reconciliation, and we harbor hatred in our hearts, sometimes for decades.

Reinhold Niebuhr composed a simple verse that came to be known as the Serenity Prayer: "God, grant me the serenity to accept the things I cannot change, the courage to change the things I can, and the wisdom to know the difference." Obviously, we cannot change the past. It is what it was and forever will be. The present, of course, is a different matter.

Today is filled with opportunities to lead, to live, to love, to work, to play, and to celebrate life. If we sincerely wish to build a better tomorrow, we can start building it today, in the present moment. So, if you've endured a difficult past, accept it, learn from it, and forgive everybody, including yourself. Once you've made peace with your past, don't spend too much time there. Instead, live in the precious present, where opportunities abound and change is still possible.

The past is history. Live in the past and you're history.
EDWIN LOUIS COLE

The past cannot be changed, but one's response to it can be.
ERWIN LUTZER

*Our yesterdays present irreparable things to us;
it is true that we have lost opportunities which will
never return, but God can transform this destructive anxiety
into a constructive thoughtfulness for the future.*
OSWALD CHAMBERS

*Trust the past to God's mercy, the present to God's love
and the future to God's providence.*
ST. AUGUSTINE

*Don't waste energy regretting the way things are or thinking
about what might have been. Start at the present moment—
accepting things exactly as they are—and search for
My way in the midst of those circumstances.*
SARAH YOUNG

*Don't be bound by the past and its failures.
But don't forget its lessons either.*
BILLY GRAHAM

MORE FROM GOD'S WORD

*One thing I do, forgetting those things which are
behind and reaching forward to those things which are ahead,
I press toward the goal for the prize of the
upward call of God in Christ Jesus.*

PHILIPPIANS 3:13–14 NKJV

*Have mercy on me, O God, according to your unfailing love;
according to your great compassion blot out my transgressions.
Wash away all my iniquity and cleanse me from my sin.*

PSALM 51:1–2 NIV

*Your old sinful self has died, and your
new life is kept with Christ in God.*

COLOSSIANS 3:3 NCV

*He restoreth my soul: he leadeth me in the
paths of righteousness for his name's sake.*

PSALM 23:3 KJV

*And He who sits on the throne said,
"Behold, I am making all things new."*

REVELATION 21:5 NASB

A TIMELY TIP FOR LEADERS

The past is past. Don't invest all your mental energy there. If you're focusing on yesterday, it's time to change your focus. And, if you're living in the past, move on while there's still time.

73
PATIENCE

A person's wisdom yields patience;
it is to one's glory to overlook an offense.
PROVERBS 19:11 NIV

Time and again, the Bible promises us that patience is its own reward, but not its only reward. Yet we human beings are, by nature, an impatient lot. We know what we want and we know when we want it: right now!

We live in an imperfect world inhabited by imperfect family members, imperfect friends, imperfect acquaintances, imperfect coworkers, and imperfect strangers. Sometimes, we inherit troubles from these imperfect people, and sometimes we create troubles for ourselves. In either case, what's required is patience—patience for other people's shortcomings as well as our own.

Proverbs 16:32 teaches, "Better to be patient than powerful; better to have self-control than to conquer a city" (NLT). But, for most of us, waiting patiently is hard. We are fallible beings who want things today, not tomorrow. Still, God instructs us to be patient and that's what we must do. It's the peaceful way to live.

Some of your greatest blessings come with patience.
WARREN WIERSBE

Bear with the faults of others as you
would have them bear with yours.
PHILLIPS BROOKS

Patience graciously, compassionately, and with understanding,
judges the faults of others without unjust criticism.
BILLY GRAHAM

Patience is the companion of wisdom.
ST. AUGUSTINE

Genius is nothing more than a
greater aptitude for patience.
BEN FRANKLIN

Delay is preferable to error.
THOMAS JEFFERSON

More from God's Word

Patience of spirit is better than haughtiness of spirit.
ECCLESIASTES 7:8 NASB

Better to be patient than powerful;
better to have self-control than to conquer a city.
PROVERBS 16:32 NLT

But if we hope for what we do not yet have,
we wait for it patiently.
ROMANS 8:25 NIV

Be joyful in hope, patient in affliction, faithful in prayer.
ROMANS 12:12 NIV

The LORD is good to those who depend on him,
to those who search for him. So it is good
to wait quietly for salvation from the LORD.
LAMENTATIONS 3:25–26 NLT

A Timely Tip for Leaders

When you learn to be a more patient leader, you'll make your world—and your heart—a better place.

74

PERSEVERANCE

*Let us not become weary in doing good, for at the proper time
we will reap a harvest if we do not give up.*
GALATIANS 6:9 NIV

Occasionally, good things happen with little or no effort. Somebody wins the lottery or inherits a fortune or stumbles onto a financial bonanza by being at the right place at the right time. But more often than not, good things happen to people who work hard, and keep working hard, when just about everybody else has gone home or given up.

Calvin Coolidge observed that, "Nothing in the world can take the place of persistence. Talent will not; . . . genius will not; . . . education will not; . . . Persistence and determination alone are omnipotent." And, President Coolidge was right. Perseverance pays.

Every marathon has a finish line, and so does yours. So keep putting one foot in front of the other, pray for strength, and don't give up. Whether you realize it or not, you're up to the challenge if you persevere. And with God's help, that's exactly what you'll do.

The Christian's journey through life
isn't a sprint but a marathon.
BILLY GRAHAM

Nothing in the world can take the place of persistence.
Talent will not; . . . genius will not; . . . education will not; . . .
Persistence and determination alone are omnipotent.
CALVIN COOLIDGE

How you respond to the challenge in the second half will
determine what you become after the game. It will determine
whether you are a winner or a loser.
LOU HOLTZ

Everyone gets discouraged. The question is:
Are you going to give up or get up? It's a choice.
JOHN MAXWELL

Perseverance is more than endurance. It is endurance
combined with absolute assurance and certainty that
what we are looking for is going to happen.
OSWALD CHAMBERS

Never give in. Never give in. Never, never, never, never—
in nothing great or small, large or petty—never give in
except to conviction of honour and good sense.
WINSTON CHURCHILL

MORE FROM GOD'S WORD

But as for you, be strong; don't be discouraged,
for your work has a reward.
2 CHRONICLES 15:7 HCSB

We are hard-pressed on every side, yet not crushed;
we are perplexed, but not in despair.
2 CORINTHIANS 4:8 NKJV

Finishing is better than starting.
Patience is better than pride.
ECCLESIASTES 7:8 NLT

For you have need of endurance, so that when you have done
the will of God, you may receive what was promised.
HEBREWS 10:36 NASB

So let us run the race that is before us and never give up.
We should remove from our lives anything that would
get in the way and the sin that so easily holds us back.
HEBREWS 12:1 NCV

A TIMELY TIP FOR LEADERS

Great leaders persevere. So if things don't work out at first, don't quit. If you don't keep trying, you'll never know how good you can be.

75

PLANNING

The wise see danger ahead and avoid it,
but fools keep going and get into trouble.
PROVERBS 22:3 NCV

If you're like most people, you probably have some sort of informal master plan for your life, a general idea of where you want to go and how you want to get there. But sometimes, informal plans aren't enough. Savvy leaders know—and the Bible makes it clear—that careful planning pays impressive dividends while impulsive decision making often does not.

Are you willing to plan for your future and work for it? And, are you willing to make God a participating partner in every aspect of that plan? If so, you can be sure that the Lord will give you strength and guide your path. So, pray about your plans, commit them to writing, and commit them to God. Then, get busy, get excited, and get ready to reap the bountiful harvest that He most certainly has in store.

*It is important to set goals because if you do not have a plan,
a goal, a direction, a purpose, and a focus, you are not going to
accomplish anything for the glory of God.*
BILL BRIGHT

*The only way you can experience abundant life
is to surrender your plans to Him.*
CHARLES STANLEY

It is better to have an ambitious plan than none at all.
WINSTON CHURCHILL

*Expect the best. Prepare for the worst.
Capitalize on what comes.*
ZIG ZIGLAR

A goal properly set is halfway reached.
ZIG ZIGLAR

*The best plan is only a plan, that is, good intentions,
unless it degenerates into work.*
PETER DRUCKER

MORE FROM GOD'S WORD

But a noble person plans noble things;
he stands up for noble causes.
ISAIAH 32:8 HCSB

Let your eyes look forward; fix your gaze straight ahead.
PROVERBS 4:25 HCSB

A wise man will listen and increase his learning,
and a discerning man will obtain guidance.
PROVERBS 1:5 HCSB

So prepare your minds for action and exercise self-control.
Put all your hope in the gracious salvation that will come
to you when Jesus Christ is revealed to the world.
1 PETER 1:13 NLT

Trust in the LORD with all your heart, and lean not
on your own understanding; in all your ways
acknowledge Him, and He shall direct your paths.
PROVERBS 3:5–6 NKJV

A TIMELY TIP FOR LEADERS

It pays to plan. As you're making plans and implementing them, consult God early (in the morning) and often (throughout the day).

76

PLEASING GOD

For merely listening to the law
doesn't make us right with God.
It is obeying the law that makes us right in his sight.
ROMANS 2:13 NLT

Sometimes, because you're an imperfect human being, you may become so wrapped up in meeting society's expectations that you fail to focus on God's expectations. To do so is a mistake of major proportions—don't make it. Instead, seek God's guidance in every aspect of your life. And, when it comes to matters of conscience, seek approval not from your peers, but from your Creator.

Whom will you try to please today? As a Christian leader, will you try to please God or man? Your primary obligation, of course, is not to please imperfect friends or casual acquaintances. Your obligation is to meet the Lord's expectations. So, turn your concerns over to Him—prayerfully, earnestly, and often. Then, listen for His answers, and trust the answers He gives.

Give me grace ever to desire and to will what is
most acceptable to thee and most pleasing in thy sight.
THOMAS À KEMPIS

To yield to God means to belong to God,
and to belong to God means to have all His infinite power.
To belong to God means to have all.
HANNAH WHITALL SMITH

Loving God—really loving Him—means living out
His commands no matter what the cost.
CHARLES COLSON

An ongoing relationship with God through His Word
is essential to the Christian's consistent victory.
BETH MOORE

Christ is not valued at all unless He is valued above all.
ST. AUGUSTINE

We may blunder on for years thinking we know
a great deal about Him, and then, perhaps suddenly,
we catch a sight of Him as He is revealed in the face
of Jesus Christ, and we discover the real God.
HANNAH WHITALL SMITH

More from God's Word

Our only goal is to please God whether we live here or there,
because we must all stand before Christ to be judged.
2 Corinthians 5:9–10 NCV

But prove yourselves doers of the word,
and not merely hearers who delude themselves.
James 1:22 NASB

Give to the Lord the glory due His name;
bring an offering, and come into His courts.
Psalm 96:8 NKJV

And it is impossible to please God without faith.
Anyone who wants to come to him must believe believe that
God exists and that he rewards those who sincerely seek him.
Hebrews 11:6 NLT

Obviously, I'm not trying to win the approval of people,
but of God. If pleasing people were my goal,
I would not be Christ's servant.
Galatians 1:10 NLT

A Timely Tip for Leaders

Being obedient to God means that you can't always please other people. So focus, first and foremost, on your relationship with the Creator. When you do, you'll find that every other relationship and every other aspect of your life will be more fulfilling.

77

POPULARITY

For am I now trying to win the favor of people, or God?
Or am I striving to please people? If I were still
trying to please people, I would not be a slave of Christ.
GALATIANS 1:10 HCSB

It feels good to be popular. That's why so many of us invest so much time, energy, and personal capital trying to gain the approval of our peers. But oftentimes, in our effort to gain earthly approval, we make spiritual sacrifices. Big mistake.

It always pays to put God first and keep Him there. When we do, our other priorities tend to fall into place. But, when we focus too intently on worldly pursuits, we suffer.

So today, as you make preparations for the day ahead, think less about pleasing people and more about pleasing your Creator. It's the best way—and the safest way—to live.

People who are not prepared to do unpopular things
and defy clamor of the multitude are not fit
to be ministers in times of difficulty.
WINSTON CHURCHILL

Popularity is far more dangerous
for the Christian than persecution.
BILLY GRAHAM

Those who follow the crowd usually get lost in it.
I don't know all the keys to success,
but one key to failure is to try to please everyone.
RICK WARREN

The major problem with letting others define you is that
it borders on idolatry. Your concern to please others
dampens your desire to please your Creator.
SARAH YOUNG

I care not what others think of what I do but, I care very much
about what I think of what I do. That is character!
THEODORE ROOSEVELT

How far would Moses have gone
if he had taken a poll in Egypt?
HARRY S TRUMAN

More from God's Word

The fear of man is a snare, but the one who
trusts in the LORD is protected.
PROVERBS 29:25 HCSB

It is better to take refuge in the LORD than to trust in man.
PSALM 118:8 HCSB

My son, if sinners entice you, don't be persuaded.
PROVERBS 1:10 HCSB

Keep your eyes focused on what is right.
and look straight ahead to what is good.
PROVERBS 4:25 NCV

Do not be unequally yoked together with unbelievers.
For what fellowship has righteousness with lawlessness?
And what communion has light with darkness?
2 CORINTHIANS 6:14 NKJV

A Timely Tip for Leaders

People who are not prepared to do unpopular things
and defy clamor of the multitude are not fit
to be ministers in times of difficulty.
WINSTON CHURCHILL

78

POSSIBILITIES

But Jesus looked at them and said to them,
"With men this is impossible,
but with God all things are possible."
MATTHEW 19:26 NKJV

The world is brimming with possibilities. And the same can be said for *your* world. You possess a unique assortment of talents and opportunities on loan from the Creator.

God has put you in a particular place, and at a specific time, of His choosing. He has an assignment that is uniquely yours, tasks that are specially intended just for you. And, whether you know it or not, He's equipped you with everything you need to fulfill His purpose and achieve His plans.

The next time you find yourself fretting about the future or worrying about things that may never come to pass, refocus your thoughts on the positive aspects of life here on earth and life eternal in heaven. And while you're at it, remember that with God all things are possible. When you let Him take over, there's simply no limit to the things that the two of you, working together, can accomplish.

*I have found that there are three
stages in every great work of God: first, it is impossible,
then it is difficult, then it is done.*
HUDSON TAYLOR

*The athlete who says that something cannot be done
should not interrupt the one who is doing it.*
JOHN WOODEN

A possibility is a hint from God.
SØREN KIERKEGAARD

*God's specialty is raising dead things to life
and making impossible things possible.
You don't have the need that exceeds His power.*
BETH MOORE

*Alleged "impossibilities" are opportunities
for our capacities to be stretched.*
CHARLES SWINDOLL

*We are all faced with a series of great opportunities
brilliantly disguised as impossible situations.*
CHARLES SWINDOLL

More from God's Word

I can do all things through Christ which strengtheneth me.
PHILIPPIANS 4:13 KJV

Jesus said to him, "If you can believe,
all things are possible to him who believes."
MARK 9:23 NKJV

The things which are impossible with men
are possible with God.
LUKE 18:27 KJV

Therefore we do not lose heart.
Even though our outward man is perishing,
yet the inward man is being renewed day by day.
2 CORINTHIANS 4:16 NKJV

Is anything too hard for the LORD?
GENESIS 18:14 KJV

A Timely Tip for Leaders

God has no limits. With Him, all things are possible. As you consider your possibilities and your plans, remember to make your heavenly Father a full partner in every endeavor.

79

PRAYER

Rejoice always, pray without ceasing,
in everything give thanks; for this is
the will of God in Christ Jesus for you.
1 THESSALONIANS 5:16–18 NKJV

Wise Christian leaders understand the power of prayer, and they never make an important decision without consulting God first. So, here's a question that was first posed by Corrie ten Boom: "Is prayer your steering wheel or your spare tire?"

Prayer is a powerful tool that you can use to change your world and change yourself. God hears every prayer and responds in His own way and according to His own timetable. When you make a habit of consulting Him about everything, He'll guide you along a path of His choosing, which, by the way, is the path you should take. And when you petition Him for strength, He'll give you the courage to face any problem and the power to meet any challenge. So today, instead of turning things over in your mind, turn them over to God in prayer. Take your concerns to the Lord and leave them there. Your heavenly Father is listening, and He wants to hear from you. Now.

Prayer is of transcendent importance. Prayer is the mightiest agent to advance God's work. Praying hearts and hands only can do God's work. Prayer succeeds when all else fails.

E. M. BOUNDS

Any concern that is too small to be turned into a prayer is too small to be made into a burden.

CORRIE TEN BOOM

Two wings are necessary to lift our souls toward God: prayer and praise. Prayer asks. Praise accepts the answer.

LETTIE COWMAN

Prayer is our lifeline to God.

BILLY GRAHAM

Don't pray when you feel like it. Have an appointment with the Lord and keep it.

CORRIE TEN BOOM

It is impossible to overstate the need for prayer in the fabric of family life.

JAMES DOBSON

MORE FROM GOD'S WORD

I desire therefore that the men pray everywhere,
lifting up holy hands, without wrath and doubting.
1 TIMOTHY 2:8 NKJV

Is anyone among you suffering? He should pray.
JAMES 5:13 HCSB

Confess your trespasses to one another, and pray for one another,
that you may be healed. The effective, fervent prayer of a
righteous man avails much.
JAMES 5:16 NKJV

And whenever you stand praying, if you have anything against
anyone, forgive him, so that your Father in heaven will also
forgive you your wrongdoing.
MARK 11:25 HCSB

Ask, and it will be given to you; seek, and you will find;
knock, and it will be opened to you.
For everyone who asks receives, and he who seeks finds,
and to him who knocks it will be opened.
MATTHEW 7:7–8 NASB

A TIMELY TIP FOR LEADERS

God does not answer all of our prayers in the affirmative. When
we are disappointed by the realities of life here on earth, we should
remember that our prayers are always answered by an all-knowing
God, and that we must trust Him, whatever the answer.

80
PRIORITIES

*Therefore, whether you eat or drink, or whatever you do,
do everything for God's glory.*
1 CORINTHIANS 10:31 HCSB

Part of every leader's job is establishing priorities—priorities for his teammates and priorities for himself. What are your priorities for the coming day and the coming year? Will you focus on your organization, your family, your finances, or your health? All these things are important, of course, but God asks you to focus on something entirely different— God asks that you focus, not on yourself or your world, but on Him.

Every morning, when you rise from bed and prepare for the coming day, the world attempts to arrange your priorities, to fill your schedule, and to crowd out God. The world says you're too busy to pray, too busy to study God's Word, and too busy to thank Him for His gifts. The world says you need noise instead of silence, entertainment instead of contemplation, constant contact instead of solitude. And, the world says that you'll stay on the right track if you simply do enough and acquire enough. But, God begs to differ. He asks that you quiet yourself each day and listen to Him. And he promises that when you listen, He will lead.

So, as you think about the things in your life that really matter— and as you establish priorities for the coming day—remember to let God lead the way. And, while you're at it, remember that the things that matter most are always the things that have eternal consequences.

Putting first things first is an issue at the very heart of life.
STEPHEN COVEY

The older I get, the more wisdom I find in the ancient rule of taking first things first—a process which often reduces the most complex human problems to manageable proportions.
DWIGHT D. EISENHOWER

The whole point of getting things done is knowing what to leave undone.
OSWALD CHAMBERS

You will not be in heaven two seconds before you cry out, why did I place so much importance on things that were so temporary? What was I thinking? Why did I waste so much time, energy and concern on what wasn't going to last?
RICK WARREN

Joy is the direct result of having God's perspective on our daily lives and the effect of loving our Lord enough to obey His commands and trust His promises.
BILL BRIGHT

Do you love life? Then do not squander time, for that's the stuff life is made of.
BEN FRANKLIN

More from God's Word

Trust in the LORD with all your heart
and lean not on your own understanding.
PROVERBS 3:5 NIV

Make yourself an example of good works
with integrity and dignity in your teaching.
TITUS 2:7 HCSB

But prove yourselves doers of the word,
and not merely hearers who delude themselves.
JAMES 1:22 NASB

For where your treasure is,
there your heart will be also.
LUKE 12:34 HCSB

He who trusts in his riches will fall,
but the righteous will flourish.
PROVERBS 11:28 NASB

A Timely Tip for Leaders

You don't have time to do everything, so it's perfectly okay to say no to the things that mean less so that you'll have time for the things that mean more. Do first things first, and keep your focus on high-priority tasks. And remember this: Your highest priority should be your relationship with your Creator and His Son.

81

PROBLEMS AND PROBLEM SOLVING

*People who do what is right may have many problems,
but the LORD will solve them all.*

PSALM 34:19 NCV

Savvy leaders recognize problems and address them as quickly as possible. But sometimes, those problems may seem too big to tackle. They are not. With God, all things are possible.

On those cloudy days when Old Man Trouble pays a visit and problems seem to be popping up everywhere, there exists a source from which we can draw perspective and courage. That source, of course, is our Creator. When we turn our troubles over to Him, we find that He is sufficient to meet our needs.

So, the next time you feel discouraged, slow down long enough to have a serious talk with your Creator. Pray for guidance, pray for strength, and pray for the wisdom to trust your heavenly Father. Your troubles are temporary; His love is not.

Each problem is a God-appointed instructor.
CHARLES SWINDOLL

Problems are the price you pay for progress.
BRANCH RICKEY

*After setting an example, the most important
component of leadership is to be a problem solver.
Problem solving is the core of leadership.*
COLIN POWELL

Human problems are never greater than divine solutions.
ERWIN LUTZER

*Faith points us beyond our problems
to the hope we have in Christ.*
BILLY GRAHAM

*A problem is nothing more
than an opportunity in work clothes.*
HENRY J. KAISER, JR.

More from God's Word

Consider it pure joy, my brothers and sisters,
whenever you face trials of many kinds, because you know
that the testing of your faith produces perseverance.
James 1:2–3 NIV

We also have joy with our troubles, because we know
that these troubles produce patience. And patience
produces character, and character produces hope.
Romans 5:3–4 NCV

Trust in the Lord with all your heart and lean not on your
own understanding; in all your ways submit to him,
and he will make your paths straight.
Proverbs 3:5–6 NIV

We are pressured in every way but not crushed;
we are perplexed but not in despair.
2 Corinthians 4:8 HCSB

I have learned in whatever state I am, to be content.
Philippians 4:11 NKJV

A Timely Tip for Leaders

Most problems aren't self-solving. So if you want to make them disappear, you'll need to spend more time praying about your problems—and working to resolve them—and less time fretting about them.

82

PURPOSE

We have also received an inheritance in Him,
predestined according to the purpose of the One who works out
everything in agreement with the decision of His will.

EPHESIANS 1:11 HCSB

Great leaders don't do things by accident, and neither does God. He didn't put you here by chance. He didn't deliver you to your particular place, at this particular time, with your particular set of talents and opportunities, on a whim. The Lord has a plan, a one-of-a-kind mission designed especially for you. Discovering that plan may take time. But if you keep asking God for guidance, He'll lead along a path of His choosing and give you every tool you need to fulfill His will.

Of course, you'll probably encounter a few impediments as you attempt to discover the exact nature of God's purpose for your life. And you may travel down a few dead ends along the way. But if you keep searching, and if you genuinely seek the Lord's guidance, He'll reveal His plans at a time and place of His own choosing.

Today and every day, God is beckoning you to hear His voice and follow His plan for your life. When you listen—and when you answer His call—you'll be amazed at the wonderful things that an all-knowing, all-powerful God can do.

*The easiest way to discover the purpose of an invention
is to ask the creator of it. The same is true for
discovering your life's purpose: Ask God.*
RICK WARREN

Live out your life in its full meaning; it is God's life.
JOSIAH ROYCE

*You weren't an accident. You weren't mass produced.
You aren't an assembly-line product. You were
deliberately planned, specifically gifted, and lovingly
positioned on the Earth by the Master Craftsman.*
MAX LUCADO

*There's some task which the God of all the universe,
the great Creator has for you to do, and which
will remain undone and incomplete, until by faith
and obedience, you step into the will of God.*
ALAN REDPATH

*All of God's people are ordinary people who have been made
extraordinary by the purpose he has given them.*
OSWALD CHAMBERS

To walk out of his will is to walk into nowhere.
C. S. LEWIS

MORE FROM GOD'S WORD

Whatever you eat or drink or whatever you do,
you must do all for the glory of God.
1 CORINTHIANS 10:31 NLT

For we are God's coworkers.
You are God's field, God's building.
1 CORINTHIANS 3:9 HCSB

For we are His creation, created in Christ Jesus
for good works, which God prepared ahead of time
so that we should walk in them.
EPHESIANS 2:10 HCSB

We must do the works of Him who sent Me while it is day.
Night is coming when no one can work.
JOHN 9:4 HCSB

And whatever you do, do it heartily,
as to the Lord and not to men.
COLOSSIANS 3:23 NKJV

A TIMELY TIP FOR LEADERS

God has big things in store for you, but He may have quite a few lessons to teach you before you are fully prepared to fulfill His purposes. So be patient, be watchful, keep working, and keep praying. Divine help is on the way.

83

QUIET TIME

*Now in the morning, having risen a long while
before daylight, He went out and departed to a solitary place;
and there He prayed.*

MARK 1:35 NKJV

Jesus understood the importance of silence. He spent precious hours alone with God, and so should we. But with our busy schedules, we're tempted to rush from place to place, checking smart phones along the way, leaving no time to contemplate spiritual matters.

You live in a noisy world, a complicated society where sights and sounds surround you and silence is in short supply. Everywhere you turn, or so it seems, the media seeks to grab your attention and hijack your thoughts. You're surrounded by big screens and little ones. And your phone can keep you logged in day and night if you let it. Don't let it.

Today and every day, you need quiet, uninterrupted time alone with God. You need to be still and listen for His voice. And, you need to seek His guidance in matters great and small. Your Creator has important plans for your day and your life. And, He's trying to get His message through. As you live and lead, you owe it to Him—and to yourself—to listen and to learn in silence.

The prayer offered to God in the morning
during your quiet time is the key that unlocks the door
of the day. Any athlete knows that it is the start
that ensures a good finish.

ADRIAN ROGERS

God's voice is still and quiet and easily buried
under an avalanche of clamor.

CHARLES STANLEY

Nothing in all creation is so like God as stillness.

GOETHE

Strength is found not in busyness and noise but in quietness.

LETTIE COWMAN

The world is full of noise. Might we not
set ourselves to learn silence, stillness, solitude?

ELISABETH ELLIOT

Fold the arms of your faith and wait in quietness
until the light goes up in your darkness.

GEORGE MACDONALD

More from God's Word

Truly my soul silently waits for God;
from Him comes my salvation.
PSALM 62:1 NKJV

Be still, and know that I am God.
PSALM 46:10 KJV

Listen in silence before me.
ISAIAH 41:1 NLT

In quietness and in confidence shall be your strength.
ISAIAH 30:15 KJV

To everything there is a season, . . . a time
to keep silence, and a time to speak.
ECCLESIASTES 3:1,7 KJV

A Timely Tip for Leaders

You live in a noisy world filled with distractions and interruptions, a world where silence is in short supply. But God wants you carve out quiet moments with Him. Silence is, indeed, golden. Value yours.

84

RENEWAL

Therefore, if anyone is in Christ,
he is a new creation; old things have passed away;
behold, all things have become new.

2 CORINTHIANS 5:17 NKJV

For busy citizens of the twenty-first century, it's easy to become overcommitted, overworked, and overstressed. If we choose, we can be connected 24-7, sparing just enough time to a few hours' sleep each night. What we need is time to renew and recharge, but where can we find the time? We can—and should—find it with God.

God can renew your strength and restore your spirits if you let Him. But He won't force you to slow down, and He won't insist that you get enough sleep at night. He leaves those choices up to you.

If you're feeling chronically tired or discouraged, it's time to rearrange your schedule, turn off the TV, power down the phone, and spend quiet time with your Creator. He knows what you need, and He wants you to experience His peace and His love. He's ready, willing, and perfectly able to renew your strength and help you prioritize the items on your to-do list if you ask Him. In fact, He's ready to hear your prayers right now. Please don't make Him wait.

God is not running an antique shop!
He is making all things new!
VANCE HAVNER

The creation of a new heart, the renewing of a right spirit is an
omnipotent work of God. Leave it to the Creator.
HENRY DRUMMOND

God specializes in giving people a fresh start.
RICK WARREN

God is in control. He may not take away trials or make
detours for us, but He strengthens us through them.
BILLY GRAHAM

Our Lord never drew power from Himself;
He drew it always from His Father.
OSWALD CHAMBERS

God will give us the strength and resources we need to live
through any situation in life that He ordains.
BILLY GRAHAM

More from God's Word

*You are being renewed in the spirit of your minds; you put
on the new self, the one created according to God's likeness in
righteousness and purity of the truth.*
EPHESIANS 4:23–24 HCSB

*Those who hope in the LORD will renew their strength.
They will soar on wings like eagles; they will run
and not grow weary, they will walk and not be faint.*
ISAIAH 40:31 NIV

*Remember ye not the former things, neither consider
the things of old. Behold, I will do a new thing.*
ISAIAH 43:18–19 KJV

*Finally, brothers, rejoice. Become mature, be encouraged,
be of the same mind, be at peace, and the God of love
and peace will be with you.*
2 CORINTHIANS 13:11 HCSB

*Now the God of all grace, who called you to His
eternal glory in Christ Jesus, will personally restore,
establish, strengthen, and support you.*
1 PETER 5:10 HCSB

A Timely Tip for Leaders

God can make all things new, including you. When you are weak
or worried, He can renew your spirit and restore your strength.
Your job, of course, is to let Him.

85

RESPONSIBILITY

So then, each of us will give an account of himself to God.
ROMANS 14:12 HCSB

God's Word encourages us to take responsibility for our actions, but the world tempts us to do otherwise. The media tries to convince us that we're "victims" of our upbringing, our government, our economic strata, or our circumstances, thus ignoring the countless blessings—and the gift of free will—that God has given each of us.

Who's responsible for your behavior? God's Word says that you are. If you obey His instructions and follow His Son, you'll be blessed in countless ways. But if you ignore the Lord's teachings, you must eventually bear the consequences of those irresponsible decisions.

Today and every day, as you make decisions about the things you'll say and do, remember who's responsible. And if you make a mistake, admit it, learn from it, and move on. The blame game has no winners; don't play.

The price of greatness is responsibility.
WINSTON CHURCHILL

*We talk about circumstances that are
"beyond our control." None of us have control over
our circumstances, but we are responsible for the way we
pilot ourselves in the midst of things as they are.*
OSWALD CHAMBERS

*Faithfulness in carrying out present duties
is the best preparation for the future.*
FRANÇOIS FÈNELON

*Action springs not from thought,
but from a readiness for responsibility.*
DIETRICH BONHOEFFER

*Firmly entrenched within every human being lies a most
deceptive presupposition: that circumstances and other people
are responsible for our own responses in life.*
ERWIN LUTZER

*No man is fit to command another
that cannot command himself.*
WILLIAM PENN

More from God's Word

But each person should examine his own work,
and then he will have a reason for boasting in himself alone,
and not in respect to someone else.
For each person will have to carry his own load.
GALATIANS 6:4–5 HCSB

Better to be patient than powerful;
better to have self-control than to conquer a city.
PROVERBS 16:32 NLT

Then He said to His disciples, "The harvest is abundant,
but the workers are few."
MATTHEW 9:37 HCSB

By their fruits ye shall know them.
MATTHEW 7:20 KJV

We must do the works of Him who sent Me while it is day.
Night is coming when no one can work.
JOHN 9:4 HCSB

A Timely Tip for Leaders

Great leaders accept responsibility for their mistakes and move on.
Poor leaders deny their mistakes and stay stuck.

86

RISK

The prudent see danger and take refuge,
but the simple keep going and pay the penalty.
PROVERBS 22:3 NIV

All the principles that you'll ever need to manage risk and live wisely can be found in a single book: the Bible. God's Word guides us along a path that leads to abundance and eternal life. When we embrace Biblical teachings and follow God's Son, we're protected. But, when we wander from His path, we inevitably suffer the consequences of our mistaken priorities.

In theory, all of us would prefer to be wise, but not all of us are willing to make the sacrifices that are required to gain real wisdom. To become wise, we must do more than spout platitudes, recite verses, or repeat aphorisms. We must not only speak wisely; we must live wisely; we must not only learn the lessons of the Christian life. We must live by them.

Today, as you think about the best way to live and way to lead, remember that God's wisdom can be found in a book that's already on your bookshelf: His Book. Read, heed, and lead accordingly.

We must combine the virtues of wisdom and of daring.
WINSTON CHURCHILL

Success cannot be guaranteed.
There are no safe battles.
WINSTON CHURCHILL

Mountain-moving faith is not just dreaming and desiring.
It is daring to risk failure.
MARY KAY ASH

Being a Christian means taking risks: risking that our love
will be rejected, misunderstood, or even ignored.
REBECCA MANLEY PIPPERT

He that would catch fish must venture his bait.
BEN FRANKLIN

You'll never reach second base if you keep one foot on first.
VERNON LAW

More from God's Word

Enthusiasm without knowledge is no good;
haste makes mistakes.
Proverbs 19:2 NLT

Spend time with the wise and you will become wise,
but the friends of fools will suffer.
Proverbs 13:20 NCV

The Lord detests the proud;
they will surely be punished.
Proverbs 16:5 NLT

But the noble make noble plans,
and by noble deeds they stand.
Isaiah 32:8 NIV

Commit your actions to the Lord,
and your plans will succeed.
Proverbs 16:3 NLT

A Timely Tip for Leaders

If you're about to make a big decision or take a significant risk, always pray about it first. And the bigger the decision, the more you should pray about it.

87

SERVICE AND SERVING GOD

The greatest among you must be a servant.
But those who exalt themselves will be humbled,
and those who humble themselves will be exalted.

MATTHEW 23:11–12 NLT

Jesus was a servant-leader, and leaders who seek to follow in His footsteps must be servants, too. But the world tries to convince us otherwise by promoting a get-ahead-at-any-cost mentality. Christian leaders, on the other had, promote a lend-a-helping-hand mentality in the workplace and beyond.

Everywhere we look, the needs are great. Whether here at home or halfway around the globe, so many people are enduring difficult circumstances. They need help, and as Christians, we are instructed to serve them.

Jesus came to this world, not to conquer, but to serve. We must do likewise by helping those who cannot help themselves. When we do, our lives will be blessed by the One who first served us.

Thinking of and serving with others can be an antidote to negative and unhealthy introspection.

BILLY GRAHAM

God wants us to serve Him with a willing spirit, one that would choose no other way.

BETH MOORE

A non-serving Christian is a contradiction in terms.

RICK WARREN

Our voices, our service, and our abilities are to be employed, primarily, for the glory of God.

BILLY GRAHAM

Faithful servants never retire. You can retire from your career, but you will never retire from serving God.

RICK WARREN

Success has nothing to do with what you gain in life or accomplish for yourself. It's what you do for others.

DANNY THOMAS

More from God's Word

Shepherd God's flock, for whom you are responsible. Watch over them because you want to, not because you are forced. That is how God wants it. Do it because you are happy to serve.
1 PETER 5:2 NCV

As each one has received a gift, minister it to one another, as good stewards of the manifold grace of God.
1 PETER 4:10 NKJV

Blessed are those servants, whom the lord when he cometh shall find watching.
LUKE 12:37 KJV

Assuredly, I say to you, inasmuch as you did it to one of the least of these My brethren, you did it to Me.
MATTHEW 25:40 NKJV

Even so faith, if it hath not works, is dead, being alone.
JAMES 2:17 KJV

A Timely Tip for Leaders

God wants you to serve Him now, not later. Jesus was a servant-leader, and if you want to follow Him, you must be a servant, too—even when service requires sacrifice.

88

SPIRITUAL GROWTH

I remind you to fan into flames
the spiritual gift God gave you.
2 TIMOTHY 1:6 NLT

As a Christian—and as a leader—you should never stop growing. No matter your age, no matter your circumstances, you have opportunities to learn and opportunities to serve. Wherever you happen to be, God is there, too, and He wants to bless you with an expanding array of spiritual gifts. Your job is to let Him.

The path to spiritual maturity unfolds day by day. Through prayer, through Bible study, through silence, and through humble obedience to God's Word, we can strengthen our relationship with Him. The more we focus on the Father, the more He blesses our lives. The more carefully we listen for His voice, the more He teaches us.

In the quiet moments when we open our hearts to the Lord, the Creator who made us keeps remaking us. He gives us guidance, perspective, courage, and strength. And the appropriate moment to accept these spiritual gifts is always the present one.

Grow, dear friends, but grow, I beseech you,
in God's way, which is the only true way.
HANNAH WHITALL SMITH

The vigor of our spiritual life will be in exact proportion to the
place held by the Bible in our life and thoughts.
GEORGE MUELLER

God's ultimate goal for your life on earth is not comfort,
but character development. He wants you to grow up spiritually
and become like Christ.
RICK WARREN

We look at our burdens and heavy loads, and we shrink from
them. But, if we lift them and bind them about our hearts, they
become wings, and on them we can rise and soar toward God.
LETTIE COWMAN

Spiritual growth doesn't happen automatically
and is rarely pretty; we will all be "under construction"
until the day we die and we finally take hold of the
"life that is truly life" (1 Tim. 6:19 NIV).
KAY WARREN

Measure your growth in grace by your sensitivity to sin.
OSWALD CHAMBERS

More from God's Word

But endurance must do its complete work, so that you may be mature and complete, lacking nothing.
James 1:4 HCSB

But grow in the grace and knowledge of our Lord and Savior Jesus Christ. To Him be the glory both now and forever. Amen.
2 Peter 3:18 NKJV

And be not conformed to this world: but be ye transformed by the renewing of your mind, that ye may prove what is that good, and acceptable, and perfect, will of God.
Romans 12:2 KJV

Leave inexperience behind, and you will live; pursue the way of understanding.
Proverbs 9:6 HCSB

So let us stop going over the basic teachings about Christ again and again. Let us go on instead and become mature in our understanding.
Hebrews 6:1 NLT

A Timely Tip for Leaders

When it comes to your faith, God doesn't want you to stand still. He wants you to keep growing. He knows that spiritual maturity is a journey, not a destination. You should know it, too.

89

STEWARDSHIP

As each one has received a gift, minister it to one another,
as good stewards of the manifold grace of God.
1 PETER 4:10 NKJV

Are you earnestly seeking God's will for your life? And do you trust His promises? If so, then you'll be a faithful steward of the resources He has entrusted you.

You possess special gifts, unique talents and opportunities that can be used or not. You should value the skills God has given you; you should nourish those talents; and you should share them with the world.

Each day provides a fresh opportunity to honor God with your prayers, with your praise, with your testimony, and with your service. Does the level of your stewardship honor the One who has given you everything? If so, rest assured: God will bless you because of your obedience. And if your stewardship has been somehow deficient, it's never too late to change. The best day to begin serving Him more faithfully is today.

All Christians are but God's stewards.
Everything we have is on loan from the Lord,
entrusted to us for a while to use in serving Him.
JOHN MACARTHUR

It is true that we may desire much more.
But let us use what we have, and God will give us more.
ADONIRAM JUDSON

We are accountable to God for the way we use our time.
BILLY GRAHAM

Do you love life? Then do not squander time,
for that's the stuff life is made of.
BEN FRANKLIN

Work is not a curse. It is the prerogative of intelligence.
CALVIN COOLIDGE

God will withdraw resources from the poor stewards,
as related in Matthew 25, and give it to the good stewards.
BILL BRIGHT

More from God's Word

His master replied, "Well done, good and faithful servant!
You have been faithful with a few things; I will
put you in charge of many things.
Come and share your master's happiness!"
MATTHEW 25:21 NIV

Be diligent that ye may be found of him in peace,
without spot, and blameless.
2 PETER 3:14 KJV

But each person should examine his own work,
and then he will have a reason for boasting in himself alone,
and not in respect to someone else. For each person
will have to carry his own load.
GALATIANS 6:4–5 HCSB

Whatever you do, do your work heartily,
as for the Lord rather than for men.
COLOSSIANS 3:23 NASB

Make a joyful noise unto the LORD, all ye lands. Serve the LORD
with gladness: come before his presence with singing.
PSALM 100:1–2 KJV

A Timely Tip for Leaders

God's Word makes it clear: During good times and hard times,
you are instructed to be a faithful steward of your talents, your
time, your leadership abilities, and your resources.

90

STRENGTH

He gives strength to the weary, and to him
who lacks might He increases power.
ISAIAH 40:29 NASB

It takes energy to be a great leader. So, where do you turn for strength when you're weary or worried? The medicine cabinet? The gym? The health food store? These places may offer a temporary energy boost, but the best place to find strength and solace isn't down the hall or at the mall; it's as near as your next breath. The best source of strength is God.

God's love for you never changes, and neither does His support. From the cradle to the grave, He has promised to give you the strength to meet the challenges of life. He has promised to guide you and protect you if you let Him. But He also expects you to do your part.

Today provides yet another opportunity to partake in the strength that only God can provide. You do so by attuning your heart to Him through prayer, obedience, and trust. Life can be challenging, but fear not. Whatever your challenge, God can give you the strength to face it and to overcome it. Let Him.

God is in control. He may not take away trials
or make detours for us,
but He strengthens us through them.
BILLY GRAHAM

The truth is, God's strength is fully revealed
when our strength is depleted.
LIZ CURTIS HIGGS

Faith is a strong power, mastering any difficulty in the
strength of the Lord who made heaven and earth.
CORRIE TEN BOOM

God will give us the strength and resources we need to live
through any situation in life that He ordains.
BILLY GRAHAM

The strength that we claim from God's Word does not
depend on circumstances. Circumstances will be difficult,
but our strength will be sufficient.
CORRIE TEN BOOM

Refuse to waste energy worrying,
and you will have strength to spare.
SARAH YOUNG

MORE FROM GOD'S WORD

The LORD is my strength and my song;
He has become my salvation.
EXODUS 15:2 HCSB

My grace is sufficient for you,
for my power is made perfect in weakness.
2 CORINTHIANS 12:9 NIV

Have faith in the LORD your God, and you will stand strong.
Have faith in his prophets, and you will succeed.
2 CHRONICLES 20:20 NCV

Be strong and courageous, and do the work.
Don't be afraid or discouraged, for the LORD God, my God,
is with you. He won't leave you or forsake you.
1 CHRONICLES 28:20 HCSB

I can do all things through Christ who strengthens me.
PHILIPPIANS 4:13 NKJV

A TIMELY TIP FOR LEADERS

Need strength? Slow down, get more rest, engage in regular, sensible exercise, and turn your troubles over to God . . . but not necessarily in that order.

91

STRESS AND REST

Come unto me, all ye that labour and are heavy laden,
and I will give you rest.
MATTHEW 11:28 KJV

You inhabit an interconnected world that never slows down and never shuts off. The world tempts you to stay up late watching the news, or surfing the Internet, or checking out social media, or gaming, or doing countless other activities that gobble up your time and distract you from more important tasks. But too much late-night screen time robs you of something you need very badly: sleep.

Are you going to bed at a reasonable hour and sleeping through the night? If so, you're both wise and blessed. But if you're staying up late with your eyes glued to a screen, you're putting your long-term health at risk. And, you're probably wasting time, too.

So, the next time you're tempted to engage in late-night time wasting, resist the temptation. Instead, turn your thoughts and prayers to God. And when you're finished, turn off the lights and go to bed. You need rest more than you need entertainment.

Life is strenuous. See that your clock does not run down.
LETTIE COWMAN

*There are many burned-out people who think
more is always better, who deem it unspiritual to say no.*
SARAH YOUNG

*Beware of having so much to do that you really do nothing at
all because you do not wait upon God to do it aright.*
C. H. SPURGEON

God specializes in giving people a fresh start.
RICK WARREN

*The more comfortable we are with mystery in our journey,
the more rest we will know along the way.*
JOHN ELDREDGE

*Prescription for a happier and healthier life:
resolve to slow your pace; learn to say no gracefully;
reject the temptation to chase after more pleasures,
more hobbies, and more social entanglements.*
JAMES DOBSON

More from God's Word

And the peace of God, which transcends all understanding,
will guard your hearts and your minds in Christ Jesus.
PHILIPPIANS 4:7 NIV

I find rest in God; only he gives me hope.
PSALM 62:5 NCV

Peace I leave with you; My peace I give to you;
not as the world gives do I give to you. Do not let
your heart be troubled, nor let it be fearful.
JOHN 14:27 NASB

You, LORD, give true peace to those who depend on you,
because they trust you.
ISAIAH 26:3 NCV

Live peaceful and quiet lives in all godliness and holiness.
1 TIMOTHY 2:2 NIV

A Timely Tip for Leaders

With God as your partner, you can overcome any obstacle. When you place your future in His hands, you have absolutely nothing to fear. The more you pray, the less stress you'll feel. So pray more and worry less. And if your fuse is chronically short, or if you're always tired, perhaps you need a little more shuteye. Try this experiment: Turn off the television and go to bed at a reasonable hour. You may be amazed at how good you feel when you get eight hours sleep.

92

THANKSGIVING

Enter into His gates with thanksgiving,
and into His courts with praise. Be thankful to Him,
and bless His name. For the LORD is good; His mercy
is everlasting, and His truth endures to all generations.
PSALM 100:4–5 NKJV

When we consider God's blessings and the sacrifices of His Son, just how thankful should we be? Should we praise our Creator once a day? Are two prayers enough? Is it sufficient that we thank our heavenly Father at mealtimes and bedtimes? The answer, of course, is no. When we consider how richly we have been blessed, now and forever—and when we consider the price Christ paid on the cross—it becomes clear that we should offer many prayers of thanks throughout the day. But all too often, amid the hustle of daily life, we forget to pause and praise the Giver of all good gifts.

Our lives expand or contract in proportion to our gratitude. When we are appropriately grateful for God's countless blessings, we experience His peace. But if we ignore His gifts, we invite stress, anxiety, and sadness into our lives.

Throughout this day, pause and say silent prayers of thanks. When you do, you'll discover that a grateful heart reaps countless blessings that a hardened heart will never know.

The Bible tells us that whenever we come before God,
whatever our purpose or prayer request,
we are always to come with a thankful heart.

DAVID JEREMIAH

It is only with gratitude that life becomes rich.

DIETRICH BONHOEFFER

Thanksgiving or complaining—these words express two
contrasting attitudes of the souls of God's children. The soul
that gives thanks can find comfort in everything; the soul that
complains can find comfort in nothing.

HANNAH WHITALL SMITH

Fill up the spare moments of your life with praise and
thanksgiving.

SARAH YOUNG

Thanksgiving will draw our hearts out to God
and keep us engaged with Him.

ANDREW MURRAY

No matter what our circumstance,
we can find a reason to be thankful.

DAVID JEREMIAH

More from God's Word

And whatever you do, in word or in deed,
do everything in the name of the Lord Jesus,
giving thanks to God the Father through Him.
Colossians 3:17 HCSB

Rejoice always, pray without ceasing, in everything give thanks;
for this is the will of God in Christ Jesus for you.
1 Thessalonians 5:16–18 NKJV

Surely the righteous shall give thanks to Your name;
the upright shall dwell in Your presence.
Psalm 140:13 NKJV

I will thank Yahweh with all my heart; I will declare
all Your wonderful works. I will rejoice and boast about You;
I will sing about Your name, Most High.
Psalm 9:1–2 HCSB

Thanks be to God for His indescribable gift.
2 Corinthians 9:15 HCSB

A Timely Tip for Leaders

Every sunrise represents yet another beautifully wrapped gift from God. Unwrap it; treasure it; use it; and give thanks to the Giver.

93

THOUGHTS

Set your mind on things above, not on things on the earth.
COLOSSIANS 3:2 NKJV

Because we are human, we are always busy with our thoughts. We simply can't help ourselves. Our brains never shut off, and even while we're sleeping, we mull things over in our minds. The question is not *if* we will think; the question is *how* we will think and *what* we will think about.

Paul Valéry observed, "We hope vaguely but dread precisely." How true. All too often, we allow the worries of everyday life to overwhelm our thoughts and cloud our vision. What's needed is clearer perspective, renewed faith, and a different focus.

When we focus on the frustrations of today or the uncertainties of tomorrow, we rob ourselves of peace in the present moment. But, when we direct our thoughts in more positive directions, we rob our worries of the power to tyrannize us.

The American poet Phoebe Cary observed, "All the great blessings of my life are present in my thoughts today." And her words apply to you. You will make your life better when you focus your thoughts on your blessings, not your misfortunes. So do yourself, your family, your friends, and your coworkers a favor: Learn to think optimistically about the world you live in and the life you lead. Then, prepare yourself for the blessings that good thoughts will bring.

Your life today is a result of your thinking yesterday. Your life tomorrow will be determined by what you think today.
JOHN MAXWELL

Change always starts in your mind.
The way you think determines the way you feel,
and the way you feel influences the way you act.
RICK WARREN

The things we think are the things that feed our souls.
If we think on pure and lovely things, we shall grow pure and lovely like them; and the converse is equally true.
HANNAH WHITALL SMITH

It is the thoughts and intents of the heart
that shape a person's life.
JOHN ELDREDGE

Most of the situations that entangle your mind are not today's concerns; you have borrowed them from tomorrow.
SARAH YOUNG

The mind is the devil's favorite avenue of attack.
BILLY GRAHAM

More from God's Word

The peace of God, which surpasses all understanding,
will guard your hearts and minds through Christ Jesus.
PHILIPPIANS 4:7 NKJV

Finally, brothers and sisters, whatever is true, whatever is
noble, whatever is right, whatever is pure, whatever is lovely,
whatever is admirable—if anything is excellent
or praiseworthy—think about such things.
PHILIPPIANS 4:8 NIV

Guard your heart above all else, for it is the source of life.
PROVERBS 4:23 HCSB

And do not be conformed to this world, but be transformed by
the renewing of your mind, so that you may prove what the will
of God is, that which is good and acceptable and perfect.
ROMANS 12:2 NASB

For to be carnally minded is death,
but to be spiritually minded is life and peace.
ROMANS 8:6 NKJV

A Timely Tip for Leaders

Unless you're willing to guard your thoughts, you'll never be able
to guard your heart. So focus on blessings, not hardships, and
opportunities, not roadblocks.

94

TODAY

*This is the day the L*ORD *has made;*
let us rejoice and be glad in it.
PSALM 118:24 HCSB

All the days on the calendar have one thing in common: They're all gifts from God. So this day, like every day, is a cause for celebration as we consider God's blessings and His love.

How will you invest this day? Will you treat your time as a commodity too precious to be squandered? Will you, as a Christian leader, carve out time during the day to serve God by serving His children? Will you celebrate God's gifts and obey His commandments? And will you share words of encouragement with the people who cross your path? The answers to these questions will determine, to a surprising extent, the quality of your day and the quality of your life.

So, wherever you find yourself today, take time to celebrate and give thanks for another priceless gift from the Father. The present moment is precious. Treat it that way.

Make each day your masterpiece.
JOHN WOODEN

The one word in the spiritual vocabulary is now.
OSWALD CHAMBERS

Today is mine. Tomorrow is none of my business. If I peer anxiously into the fog of the future, I will strain my spiritual eyes so that I will not see clearly what is required of me now.
ELISABETH ELLIOT

Yesterday is the tomb of time, and tomorrow is the womb of time. Only now is yours.
R. G. LEE

It is a mistake to look too far ahead. Only one link in the chain of destiny can be handled at a time.
WINSTON CHURCHILL

How ridiculous to grasp for future gifts when today's is set before you. Receive today's gift gratefully, unwrapping it tenderly and delving into its depths.
SARAH YOUNG

MORE FROM GOD'S WORD

But encourage each other every day while it is "today."
Help each other so none of you will become hardened
because sin has tricked you.
HEBREWS 3:13 NCV

So don't worry about tomorrow, because tomorrow will have
its own worries. Each day has enough trouble of its own.
MATTHEW 6:34 NCV

There is a time for everything,
and a season for every activity under heavens.
ECCLESIASTES 3:1 NIV

The world and its desires pass away,
but whoever does the will of God lives forever.
1 JOHN 2:17 NIV

So teach us to number our days, that we may
present to You a heart of wisdom.
PSALM 90:12 NASB

A TIMELY TIP FOR LEADERS

Today is a wonderful, one-of-a-kind gift from God. Treat it that way.

95

TRUSTING GOD

Trust in the LORD with all your heart, and lean not
on your own understanding; in all your ways
acknowledge Him, and He shall direct your paths.
PROVERBS 3:5–6 NKJV

As we pass through this world, we travel past peaks and valleys. When we reach the mountaintops of life, we find it easy to praise God and to give thanks. And as we reach the crest of the mountain's peak, we find it easy to trust God's plan. But, when we find ourselves in the dark valleys of life, when we face disappointment, despair, or heartbreak, it's much more difficult to trust God. Yet, trust Him we must.

As Christians, we can be comforted: Whether we find ourselves at the pinnacle of the mountain or the darkest depths of the valley, God is there. And, we Christians have every reason to live courageously. After all, Christ has already won the ultimate battle on the cross at Calvary.

So, the next time you find your courage tested to the limit, lean upon God's promises. Trust His Son. Remember that God is always near and that He is your protector and your deliverer. When you are worried, anxious, or afraid, call upon Him. God can handle your problems infinitely better than you can, so turn them over to Him. Remember that God rules both mountaintops and valleys—with limitless wisdom and love—now and forever.

Never imagine that you can be a loser by trusting in God.
C. H. SPURGEON

Never yield to gloomy anticipation. Place your hope and confidence in God. He has no record of failure.
LETTIE COWMAN

Faith and obedience are bound up in the same bundle. He that obeys God, trusts God; and he that trusts God, obeys God.
C. H. SPURGEON

One of the marks of spiritual maturity is the quiet confidence that God is in control, without the need to understand why he does what he does.
CHARLES SWINDOLL

When trust is perfect and there is no doubt, prayer is simply the outstretched hand ready to receive.
E. M. BOUNDS

To know the will of God is the highest of all wisdom.
BILLY GRAHAM

More from God's Word

In quietness and trust is your strength.
ISAIAH 30:15 NASB

*The LORD is my rock, my fortress, and my deliverer, my God,
my mountain where I seek refuge. My shield, the horn of my
salvation, my stronghold, my refuge, and my Savior.*
2 SAMUEL 22:2–3 HCSB

*The fear of man is a snare, but the one
who trusts in the Lord is protected.*
PROVERBS 29:25 HCSB

*Those who trust in the LORD are like Mount Zion.
It cannot be shaken; it remains forever.*
PSALM 125:1 HCSB

*Jesus said, "Don't let your hearts be troubled.
Trust in God, and trust in me."*
JOHN 14:1 NCV

A Timely Tip for Leaders

Because God is trustworthy—and because He has made promises
to you that He intends to keep—you are protected. The Lord
always keeps His promises. Trust Him.

96

TRUTH

You will know the truth,
and the truth will set you free.
JOHN 8:32 HCSB

God is vitally concerned with truth. His Word teaches the truth; His Spirit reveals the truth; His Son leads us to the truth. When we open our hearts to the Lord, and when we allow His Son to rule over our hearts and our lives, God reveals Himself, and we come to understand the truth about ourselves and the Truth (with a capital T) about His grace.

The familiar words of John 8:32 remind us that when we come to know God's Truth, we are liberated. Have you been liberated by that Truth? And are you living in accordance with the unchanging promises that you find in God's Holy Word? Hopefully so.

Today, as you fulfill the responsibilities that the Lord has placed before you, ask yourself this question: "Do my thoughts and actions bear witness to the ultimate truth that God has placed on my heart, or am I allowing the stresses of everyday life to overwhelm me?" It's a profound question that deserves a truthful answer . . . *now.*

*I never tell my players anything
I don't absolutely believe myself.*
VINCE LOMBARDI

Those who walk in truth walk in liberty.
BETH MOORE

*We have in Jesus Christ a perfect example
of how to put God's truth into practice.*
BILL BRIGHT

We learn his truth by obeying it.
OSWALD CHAMBERS

*Truth will triumph. The Father of truth will win,
and the followers of truth will be saved.*
MAX LUCADO

*The greatest friend of truth is time, her greatest enemy
is prejudice, and her constant companion humility.*
CHARLES COLSON

More from God's Word

When the Spirit of truth comes,
He will guide you into all the truth.
JOHN 16:13 HCSB

Jesus said, "I am the Road, also the Truth, also the Life.
No one gets to the Father apart from me."
JOHN 14:6 MSG

But do not follow foolish stories that disagree with God's truth,
but train yourself to serve God.
1 TIMOTHY 4:7 NCV

Learn the truth and never reject it.
Get wisdom, self-control, and understanding.
PROVERBS 23:23 NCV

Teach me Your way, O LORD; I will walk in Your truth.
PSALM 86:11 NASB

A Timely Tip for Leaders

Jesus offers you the Truth with a Capital T. How you respond to His Truth will determine the direction—and the destination—of your life.

97

VALUES

The righteousness of the blameless clears his path, but the wicked person will fall because of his wickedness.
PROVERBS 11:5 HCSB

Great leaders know where they stand and what they stand for. They know the values that matter most, and they live by them. And, they communicate those values to their coworkers and teammates.

God's Word teaches us how to live; it tells us what to do and what not to do. As Christians we are called to walk with God's Son and to obey God's commandments. But, we live in a world that presents us with many temptations, each of which has the potential to distract us or destroy us.

Charles Swindoll correctly observed, "Nothing speaks louder or more powerfully than a life of integrity." Wise leaders agree. So, as you establish the set of values that you'll live by—and lead by— make the Bible your guidebook. When you do, you'll be protected and you'll be blessed.

When you live in the light of eternity, your values change.
RICK WARREN

*Our system of values becomes the navigating system
that guides us. It establishes priorities in our lives
and judges what we will accept or reject.*
JOHN MAXWELL

*The human mind has no more power of inventing a
new value than of planting a new sun in the sky or a new
primary color in the spectrum.*
C. S. LEWIS

*The Reference Point for the Christian is the Bible.
All values, judgments, and attitudes must be gauged
in relationship to this Reference Point.*
RUTH BELL GRAHAM

We glorify God by living lives that honor Him.
BILLY GRAHAM

*Eternal values, not temporal ones, should become
the deciding factors for your decisions.*
RICK WARREN

More from God's Word

*So I strive always to keep my conscience
clear before God and man.*
ACTS 24:16 NIV

*Let us come near to God with a sincere heart and a sure faith,
because we have been made free from a guilty conscience, and
our bodies have been washed with pure water.*
HEBREWS 10:22 NCV

*If then you were raised with Christ, seek those things which
are above, where Christ is, sitting at the right hand of God.
Set your mind on things above, not on things on the earth.*
COLOSSIANS 3:1–2 NKJV

*Do not conform to the pattern of this world,
but be transformed by the renewing of your mind.
Then you will be able to test and approve what God's will is—
his good, pleasing and perfect will.*
ROMANS 12:2 NIV

*The integrity of the upright guides them, but the
perversity of the treacherous destroys them.*
PROVERBS 11:3 HCSB

A Timely Tip for Leaders

Before you make a big decision, think about the things you stand
for. And be sure that your choices are consistent with your values.

98

WISDOM AND UNDERSTANDING

The fear of the LORD is the beginning of knowledge,
but fools despise wisdom and instruction.
PROVERBS 1:7 NKJV

What makes a wise leader? Training, of course. And experience. And judgment. And common sense. But all these things, valuable though they may be, aren't enough. Genuine wisdom begins with God's Word.

Savvy leaders know that the search for wisdom is a lifelong journey. We should continue to read, to watch, to test our assumptions, and to learn new things as long as we live. But it's not enough to learn new things or to memorize the great Biblical truths; we must also live by them.

So, what will you learn today? Will you take time to feed your mind and fill your heart? And will you study the guidebook that God has given you? Hopefully so, because His plans and His promises are waiting for you there, inside the covers of a book like no other: His Book. It contains the essential wisdom you'll need to navigate the seas of life and land safely on that distant shore.

The more wisdom enters our hearts,
the more we will be able to
trust our hearts in difficult situations.
JOHN ELDREDGE

Wisdom is the right use of knowledge. To know
is not to be wise. There is no fool so great as the knowing fool.
But, to know how to use knowledge is to have wisdom.
C. H. SPURGEON

Knowledge is horizontal. Wisdom is vertical;
it comes down from above.
BILLY GRAHAM

Wisdom is the power to see and the inclination
to choose the best and highest goal,
together with the surest means of attaining it.
J. I. PACKER

Knowledge is not wisdom.
Wisdom is the proper use of knowledge.
VANCE HAVNER

MORE FROM GOD'S WORD

Get wisdom—how much better it is than gold!
And get understanding—it is preferable to silver.
PROVERBS 16:16 HCSB

But the wisdom that is from above is first pure, then peaceable,
gentle, willing to yield, full of mercy and good fruits,
without partiality and without hypocrisy.
JAMES 3:17 NKJV

He that walketh with wise men shall be wise:
but a companion of fools shall be destroyed.
PROVERBS 13:20 KJV

But if any of you lacks wisdom, let him ask of God,
who gives to all generously and without reproach,
and it will be given to him.
JAMES 1:5 NASB

Who among you is wise and understanding? Let him show by
his good behavior his deeds in the gentleness of wisdom.
JAMES 3:13 NASB

A TIMELY TIP FOR LEADERS

If you're looking for wisdom, the book of Proverbs is a wise place to start. It has thirty-one chapters, one for each day of the month. When you read Proverbs and take its teachings to heart, you'll gain timeless wisdom from God's unchanging Word.

99
WORK

Whatever you do, do it enthusiastically,
as something done for the Lord and not for men.
COLOSSIANS 3:23 HCSB

Time and again, the Bible extolls the value of hard work. In Proverbs, we are instructed to take a lesson from a surprising source: ants. Ants are among nature's most industrious creatures. They do their work without supervision, hesitation, or complaint. We should do likewise, but oftentimes we don't. We're tempted to look for shortcuts (there aren't any), or we rely on luck (it happens, but we shouldn't depend on it). Meanwhile, the clock continues to tick, life continues to pass, and important work goes undone.

The book of Proverbs proclaims, "One who is slack in his work is brother to one who destroys" (18:9 NIV). And in his second letter to the Thessalonians, Paul writes, "If any would not work, neither should he eat" (3:10 KJV). And. In short, God has created a world in which labor is rewarded but laziness is not.

As you think about the way you lead and the way you work, please remember that God has big plans for you, and He's given you everything you need to fulfill His purpose. But He won't force His plans upon you, and He won't do all the work. He expects you to do your part. When you do, you'll earn the rewards He most certainly has in store.

God did not intend for us to be idle and unproductive.
There is dignity in work.
BILLY GRAHAM

What is needed for happy effectual service is simply to put your
work into the Lord's hand, and leave it there.
HANNAH WHITALL SMITH

Success or failure can be pretty well predicted
by the degree to which the heart is fully in it.
JOHN ELDREDGE

Work isn't only earning a living; work gives us a sense of
purpose, and worth, and opportunities for companionship.
BILLY GRAHAM

Work as if you were to live a hundred years.
Pray as if you were to die tomorrow.
BEN FRANKLIN

Think of something you ought to do and go do it.
Heed not your feelings. Do your work.
GEORGE MACDONALD

More from God's Word

*But this I say: He who sows sparingly will also reap sparingly,
and he who sows bountifully will also reap bountifully.*
2 CORINTHIANS 9:6 NKJV

*Be strong and courageous, and do the work.
Don't be afraid or discouraged, for the LORD God, my God,
is with you. He won't leave you or forsake you.*
1 CHRONICLES 28:20 HCSB

*The plans of hard-working people earn a profit,
but those who act too quickly become poor.*
PROVERBS 21:5 NCV

*Do you see a man skilled in his work?
He will stand in the presence of kings.*
PROVERBS 22:29 HCSB

*I must work the works of Him who sent Me while it is day;
the night is coming when no one can work.*
JOHN 9:4 NKJV

A Timely Tip for Leaders

Here's a time-tested formula for success: Have faith in God and do the work. Hard work is not simply a proven way to get ahead, it's also part of God's plan for all His children (including you).

100

WORLDLINESS

*And do not be conformed to this world, but be transformed by
the renewing of your mind, that you may prove what is that
good and acceptable and perfect will of God.*

ROMANS 12:2 NKJV

We live in this world, but we should not worship it. Yet, we are bombarded by messages and distractions that tempt us to do otherwise. The twenty-first-century world in which we live is a noisy, confusing place. The world seems to cry, "Worship me with your money, your time, your energy, your thoughts, and your life." But if we are wise, we won't worship the world; we will worship God.

If you wish to build your character day by day, you must distance yourself, at least in part, from the temptations and distractions of modern-day society. But distancing yourself isn't easy, especially when so many societal forces are struggling to capture your attention, your participation, and your money.

All of mankind is engaged in a colossal, worldwide treasure hunt. Some people seek treasure from earthly sources; others seek God's treasures by making Him the cornerstone of their lives. What kind of treasure hunter are you? Are you so caught up in the demands of everyday living that you sometimes allow the search for worldly treasures to become your primary focus? If so, it's time to reorganize your daily to-do list by placing God in His rightful place:

first place. Don't allow anyone or anything to separate you from your heavenly Father and His only begotten Son.

Worldliness is an inner attitude that puts
self at the center of life instead of God.
BILLY GRAHAM

We live in a hostile world that constantly
seeks to pull us away from God.
BILLY GRAHAM

Loving the world destroys our relationship with God,
it denies our faith in God, and it
discounts our future with God.
DAVID JEREMIAH

The voices of the world are a cacophony of chaos, pulling you
this way and that. Don't listen to those voices.
SARAH YOUNG

We need more love for the word and less love for the world.
R. G. LEE

If you are a Christian, you are not a citizen of this world
trying to get to heaven; you are a citizen of heaven
making your way through this world.
VANCE HAVNER

More from God's Word

*For our citizenship is in heaven, from which also we
eagerly wait for a Savior, the Lord Jesus Christ.*
PHILIPPIANS 3:20 NASB

*No one can serve two masters. For you will hate one and love
the other; you will be devoted to one and despise the other.
You cannot serve God and be enslaved to money.*
LUKE 16:13 NLT

*Do you not know that friendship with the world
is hostility toward God? So whoever wants to be
the world's friend becomes God's enemy.*
JAMES 4:4 HCSB

*Set your mind on the things above,
not on the things that are on earth.*
COLOSSIANS 3:2 NASB

*Pure and undefiled religion before our God and Father is this:
to look after orphans and widows in their distress and to keep
oneself unstained by the world.*
JAMES 1:27 HCSB

A Timely Tip for Leaders

If you're determined to be a faithful follower of the One from Galilee,
you must make certain that you focus on His values, not society's
values—and those two sets of values are almost never the same.

MORE GREAT IDEAS FOR LEADERS

About Achievement

*Your own resolution to success
is more important than any other thing.*
ABRAHAM LINCOLN

*Think of yourself as on the threshold of unparalleled success.
A whole, clear, glorious life lies before you.*
ANDREW CARNEGIE

*Don't measure yourself by what you have accomplished but by
what you should have accomplished with your ability.*
JOHN WOODEN

*What is the recipe for successful achievement? Choose a
career you love. Give it the best there is in you. Seize your
opportunities. And be a member of the team.*
BEN FRANKLIN

*Diligence overcomes difficulties;
sloth makes them.*
BEN FRANKLIN

Never mistake activity for achievement.
JOHN WOODEN

ABOUT ADVERSITY

In a crisis, don't hide behind anything or anybody.
They're going to find you anyway.
BEAR BRYANT

It's our duty to make the best of misfortunes.
GEORGE WASHINGTON

Show me someone who has done something worthwhile,
and I'll show you someone who has overcome adversity.
LOU HOLTZ

Difficulties mastered are opportunities won.
WINSTON CHURCHILL

First, remember that no matter how bad a situation is,
it's not as bad as you think.
COLIN POWELL

About Character

Ability may take you to the top,
but it takes character to keep you there.
JOHN WOODEN

Character is like a tree and reputation like its shadow.
The shadow is what we think; the tree is the real thing.
ABRAHAM LINCOLN

No amount of ability is of the slightest avail without honor.
ANDREW CARNEGIE

Show class, have pride, and display character.
If you do, winning takes care of itself.
BEAR BRYANT

A sound body is good; a sound mind is better;
but, a strong and clean character is better than either.
THEODORE ROOSEVELT

The ultimate measure of a man is not
where he stands in moments of comfort, but where he stands
at times of challenge and controversy.
MARTIN LUTHER KING JR.

About Decisions

When confronted with a decision, write down the pros and cons, cancel them out one against the other, then take the course indicated by what remains.

BEN FRANKLIN

There is, therefore, wisdom in reserving one's decisions as long as possible and until all the facts that we believe to be important at the moment are revealed.

WINSTON CHURCHILL

To get the facts first is often impossible. Those who make effective decisions must start with informed opinions.

PETER DRUCKER

Decision making is the specific executive task.

PETER DRUCKER

There is a precipice on either side of you— a precipice of caution and a precipice of over-daring.

WINSTON CHURCHILL

Whenever you see a successful business, someone made a courageous decision.

PETER DRUCKER

ABOUT OPPORTUNITY

*To succeed, jump as quickly at opportunities
as you do at conclusions.*
BEN FRANKLIN

Never surrender opportunity to security.
BRANCH RICKEY

*Opportunity is missed by most people because
it is dressed in overalls and looks like work.*
HENRY J. KAISER, JR.

*An organization will have a high spirit of performance
if it is consistently directed toward opportunity
rather than toward problems.*
PETER DRUCKER

Difficulties mastered are opportunities won.
WINSTON CHURCHILL

Nine-tenths of wisdom is being wise in time.
THEODORE ROOSEVELT

ABOUT PERSEVERANCE

Always bear in mind that your own resolution to succeed is more important than any one thing.
ABRAHAM LINCOLN

Energy and persistence alter all things.
BEN FRANKLIN

Never give in. Never give in. Never, never, never, never—in nothing, great or small, large or petty—never give in, except to convictions of honour and good sense.
WINSTON CHURCHILL

When you get to the end of your rope, tie a knot and hang on.
FRANKLIN D. ROOSEVELT

Nothing in the world can take the place of persistence. Talent will not; genius will not; education will not. Persistence and determination alone are omnipotent.
CALVIN COOLIDGE

ABOUT SUCCESS

Think of yourself as on the threshold of unparalleled success.
A whole, clear, glorious life lies before you.
ANDREW CARNEGIE

Morale and attitude are the fundamental ingredients to success.
BUD WILKINSON

Success is the result of hard work,
learning from failure, loyalty, and persistence.
COLIN POWELL

The key to success? Understanding that there's no free lunch.
LOU HOLTZ

Success has nothing to do with what you gain in life or
accomplish for yourself. It's what you do for others.
DANNY THOMAS

Real success consists in doing one's duty well
in the path where one's life is led.
THEODORE ROOSEVELT

About Winning and Losing

First become a winner in life. Then it's easier to become a winner on the field.

TOM LANDRY

Show class, have pride, and display character. If you do, winning takes care of itself.

BEAR BRYANT

Although I wanted my players to work to win, I tried to convince them they had always won when they had done their best.

JOHN WOODEN

You can learn a line from a win. You can learn a book from a defeat.

PAUL BROWN

Losing doesn't make you a loser unless you think you're a loser.

MIKE KRZYZEWSKI

The price of victory is high, but so are the rewards.

BEAR BRYANT

ABOUT WORK

Work as if you were to live a hundred years.
Pray as if you were to die tomorrow.
BEN FRANKLIN

The harder you work, the harder it is to surrender.
VINCE LOMBARDI

Work is a good word. When we work hard at something we
enjoy and feel good about, we feel better about ourselves.
MIKE KRZYZEWSKI

Dreams never hurt anybody who kept working right behind
the dream to make as much of it come true as possible.
F. W. WOOLWORTH

A dream doesn't become reality through magic;
it takes sweat, determination and hard work.
COLIN POWELL

Nothing will work unless you do.
JOHN WOODEN